OF MEN AND SHIPS

OF MEN

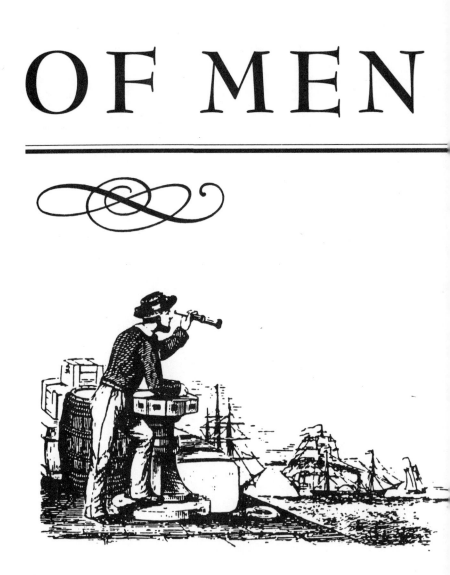

AND SHIPS

The Best Sea Tales

SCOTT RYE

· LONGMEADOW · PRESS ·

Cover design by Mike Stromberg
Interior design by Bernard Schleifer

Library of Congress Cataloging-in-Publication Data

Rye, Scott.
Of men and ships : the best sea tales / Scott Rye.
—1st ed. p.   cm.
ISBN: 0-681-41817-6
1. Seafaring life.   I. Title.
G540.R83   1993
910.4′5—dc20   92-44753
CIP

Printed in United States of America
FIRST EDITION
0 9 8 7 6 5 4 3 2 1

For
Ruth and Victoria

A C K N O W L E D G M E N T S

I'D LIKE TO THANK some of the people who made this book possible, starting with Mr. T.J. "Jocko" Potts, who originated "Of Men & Ships" in 1973; my agent at William Morris Agency, Mr. Matt Bialer; Ms. Pam Altschul Liflander, my editor at Longmeadow; Ms. Emma Campbell, who helped prepare the manuscript; and my lovely wife, Ruth, who proofed the manuscript and provided much-needed support.

CONTENTS

The Somers Affair   15

Paddy Gilroy Takes On the Yanks   31

The Icebound Voyage of the Fram   39

A Decade of Splendor, Speed, and Sail   49

The Wireless Proves Itself   55

The Indomitable Admiral Benbow   63

The Ship that Met Herself in Battle   71

The Legend Behind Moby Dick   81

Across the Pacific in a Longboat   89

The Gentlemanly War of Commander Karl von Müller   95

The Forgotten Admiral Blake   111

Forty Fathoms Down   119

Captain Mad Jack Percival   129

George Tilton's Long Hike for Help   137

The Loss of Lord Kitchener   143

The Texas Navy   153

Nelson's First Taste of Glory   163

Across the Atlantic in a Flying Boat   173

Navarino—End of an Era   181

A Matter of Endurance   187

Revenue Cutters and the Battle of New Orleans   195

The Cruise of the Sea Devil   205

The Thin Gray Line   215

The "Ever Unlucky" Pandora   225

Lieutenant Izac's Great Escape   237

The Waving Girl of Savannah   247

PREFACE

How does it ever happen? A brief glimpse here, a quick flirtation. A slow seduction that begins with curiosity, develops into respect and admiration, and finally matures into something greater. Perhaps it was those first trips to the glistening white sands and crystalline waters of the Gulf of Mexico so long ago. Maybe it was the first time my father allowed me to take the helm of our Scandinavian-built cruiser. Whatever started it, I found myself fascinated by the sea and all things nautical. The shelves of the room of my youth bristled with models of ships, dozens of shells and starfish, bits of coral, and other treasures gathered along the shores of the ocean.

Reading did a great deal to stoke the fires of my imagination, starting with C. S. Forester's wonderful Horatio Hornblower series. Some of the greatest literature in the English language centers around life at sea—Melville's masterpieces, *Moby Dick*, *Typee*, and *Billy Budd*; Nordhoff and Hall's *Mutiny on the Bounty*; Wouk's *The Caine Mutiny*; among others. The works of Joseph Conrad stand apart, not only as examples of excellent nautical pieces, but as some of the finest writing ever published.

And, as exciting as the adventures of Admiral Lord Hornblower, Mr. Midshipman Easy, Captain Blood, Lord Jim, Marlow, and

Captain Ahab are to countless readers and moviegoers, the stories of real-life seafarers are even more compelling. Here are men who lived the adventure—who have known the exhilaration of discovery, the stark terror of battle at sea, the daily rigors of the sailor's life, as well as the pleasures of distant ports. These are men for whom a predictable, safe existence on land held no appeal, rugged individuals who routinely overcame seemingly insurmountable odds to achieve victory, however fleeting.

Some of the names in this book will be familiar: Lord Nelson, Jean Lafitte, Lord Kitchener; others will not be–Count Felix von Luckner, Captain Alexander Slidell Mackenzie, Jack Binns. Yet the stories recounted here concern flesh-and-blood humans, otherwise ordinary people performing extraordinary feats. Here are a handful of survivors of a merchant ship sailing 4,000 miles across the Pacific in an open boat; here is Dr. Fridtjof Nansen, purposely trapping his ship in the Arctic ice in an effort to be the first to reach the North Pole; here are the pioneer naval aviators who were the first to fly across the Atlantic. This book is not intended as a history; rather, it provides glimpses of the men who ventured forth on the far-flung oceans of the world and the adventures they found.

This collection is a sampling taken from the "Of Men & Ships" feature that appears monthly in *Port of Mobile* magazine. A female naval officer friend once suggested changing the name of the column to something less discriminatory, such as "Of Men, Women & Ships," or "Of Ships and the Sea," but, tradition aside (the feature has appeared regularly since March 1973), the simple fact is that seafaring historically has been a man's profession.

A year ago, while visiting this magnificent house, which is reminiscent of something out of a Somerset Maugham story, my host asked if I thought I could write here. That brief visit rejuvenated my spirit and sparked the idea for several pieces, and I have looked forward to my return to work on this collection.

The house commands a view of Goodman Bay, the beach of which sweeps around in a sharp, white crescent to the Crystal

Palace. From my white wicker rocker on the second-story porch I can see two Bahamian-rigged sailboats anchored in the beds of seagrass, and beyond, the topaz blue of clear water. Perhaps a quarter-mile out surf breaks on the reef. Farther out, where sport fishermen troll, the water takes on a darker mantle. Balmoral Island lies to the northwest of the house, and to the northeast, seen through the feathery needles of Australian pines, great cruise ships stand out from Nassau. It is an inspiring setting, and I am grateful to my host, Mr. Matt Metcalfe, for the opportunity to stay here and work among the sights and sounds of the sea and the delights of coconut palms, hibiscus, and bougainvillea.

I would also like to express my thanks to my boss, Mr. Bill Yeager, and our clients at the Alabama State Docks, Director John Dutton, Mr. Buddy Browning, Ms. Sarah Teague, and Ms. Sue Alexander, who allow me carte blanche in writing "Of Men & Ships." I owe a great deal to my art director, M. Jerry Peloux, a native of the South Pacific who has been researching and illustrating "Of Men & Ships" since long before I was ever involved with the magazine. I also appreciate the kind words of all the people who encouraged me to put together a few of these stories, especially Colonel Herb Lockett, who seems to have led the charge.

Soon I will be back home, and that's all right. From outside my office I can see ships coming and going, smell their exhaust, and hear the sounds of the busy waterfront. Before too long I will embark upon another adventure, retracing an ancient journey, battling with ruthless pirates or exploring the unknown—always fortunate enough to be sailing with the best of men and ships.

Scott Rye
December 31, 1991
"Bienvenida"
New Providence Island
Bahamas

The *Somers* Affair

MIDSHIPMAN PHILIP SPENCER stood abaft the gangway, hesitating to give the most difficult order he could ever imagine. Members of the ship's crew shifted their weight uneasily in the silence. Finally, Spencer turned to a boatswain's mate and said he could not bring himself to give the order. The ship's captain, Commander Alexander Slidell Mackenzie, stepped forward and commanded, "Stand by . . . fire!" As a cannon on deck roared, Midshipman Philip Spencer and two others were jerked skyward from the deck, hanged for plotting a mutiny aboard the *U.S.S. Somers*.

The hanging of the three on December 1, 1842, ended a tense six days on board the training brig *Somers*, but Captain Mackenzie's ordeal was just beginning. The hangings were unprecedented in U.S. Navy history, and Mackenzie had clearly overstepped his legal boundaries by hanging the alleged mutineers without a court-martial. When the brig docked in New York thirteen days later and word of the mutinous plot and subsequent hangings became public knowledge, Commander Mackenzie was simultaneously heralded as a hero and a villain. He soon found himself fighting for his own life.

Alexander Mackenzie Slidell was born the son of a tallow chandler in New York. His older sister, Jane, married Lieutenant Matthew C. Perry whose older brother, the famed Oliver Hazard Perry, secured a warrant as midshipman for Alex Slidell. He entered the service at age eleven and was promoted to lieutenant at the age of twenty or twenty-one and, while on a cruise in the West Indies, contracted yellow fever. As part of his convalescence, the young officer traveled to Europe where he fell in with literary society, including Washington Irving and Henry Wadsworth Longfellow.

Slidell managed to split his time between his two professions—naval officer and well-respected author—during the next few years. In the late 1830s he reversed his middle and surnames at the request of a wealthy Scottish uncle who did not wish to see the family name of Mackenzie die.

Now officially known as Mackenzie, the officer gained command of the schooner *U.S.S. Dolphin* and was promoted to commander in 1841. He then assumed command of the steam sloop *Missouri*. In the spring of 1842, he was given command of a new brig, the *U.S.S. Somers*, which was to serve as a training ship for young apprentices.

One of the "young gentlemen" assigned to the *Somers* was Acting Midshipman Philip Spencer. Spencer's connections were no less illustrious than his captain's. His uncle was a Navy captain, his father had been Chief Justice of the New York Supreme Court, and his father was John C. Spencer, U.S. secretary of war. Young Spencer had proven to be the black sheep of the family, however. He had spent three years as a freshman at Geneva College before being sent to Union College, his father's alma mater, where he accomplished little in his few short weeks except to found the fraternity Chi Psi. By summer his father had grown tired of his son's tomfoolery and drinking bouts and decided that the Navy might teach him some discipline.

Despite the rigors of Navy life, Acting Midshipman Spencer still refused to flourish. His record notes drunkenness and insubordination, and he went as far as using his father's cabinet post to threaten his superiors. He was soon asked to resign his commission, but Secretary Spencer was able to have his son's rank restored. The elder

Midshipman Philip Spencer, allegedly plotted to seize control of the United States Ship Somers.

Spencer agreed to give his son one last chance. His assignment to the *Somers* would prove to be his last.

Designed to carry a complement of ninety, the *Somers* sailed with 120 officers and men, eighty-nine of whom were boys between the ages of thirteen and nineteen. The seven midshipmen on board ranged in age from sixteen to twenty years old. The only line officers aboard were Commander Mackenzie and his executive officer, Lieutenant Guert Gansevoort. Other officers included Passed Assistant Surgeon R. W. Leecock; Purser H. M. Heiskill, and Mackenzie's nephew, Acting Master M. C. Perry. Another nephew, O. H. Perry, did midshipman's duty and served as captain's clerk.

Spencer was disliked by his fellow junior officers. He was a surly and lazy eighteen-year-old, given to daydreaming. According to earlier acquaintances, Spencer had spent much of his time in college reading pirate novels and had boasted to several people that some day he would become a famous pirate. He had also toyed with the ideas of going west and becoming a highwayman or a "buccaneer on the Mississippi." His life at sea, however, had been anything but adventurous. The *Somers'* duty was to carry out a practice cruise and deliver packages to the *U.S.S. Vandalia*. She sailed as far as the west coast of Africa without sighting the *Vandalia* and then turned her bow toward the warm waters of the West Indies.

All seemed well enough aboard the brig. Although floggings were fairly common, the captain shrugged off his crew's sometimes unruly behavior as the excesses of youth. Spencer cavorted with the boys more and more often and fell in with the boatswain's mate, Samuel Cromwell, and an ordinary seaman, Elisha Small. Spencer coerced a steward into stealing brandy from the galley, and he was often seen huddled with these two rather unsavory sailors, smoking cigars. Even with Spencer's questionable behavior, however, there was nothing to suggest a budding mutiny on the *Somers*.

Then, on the night of November 25, 1842, Midshipman Spencer approached Purser's Steward J. W. Wales. After some small talk about the weather, Spencer asked Wales if he were afraid to die and if he thought he could kill a man if necessary. Taken aback by the questions, Wales managed to answer that he was in no hurry to die but was not afraid of death, and, if necessary, he thought that he could kill someone.

Spencer then sketched out his intention to lead a mutiny, kill the other officers, and turn the *Somers* into a pirate ship. According to Wales's later testimony, Spencer talked to him for more than half an hour, explaining how the ship could be taken. Spencer called to Seaman Small and spoke to him in Spanish, adding in English that Wales was on their side. The midshipman offered Wales a post as third officer on the pirate ship. Fearing for his life, Wales pretended to accept the position. Spencer warned Wales that if he gave away the plot he would be killed by the midshipman or one of his confederates.

Wales didn't know what to do. He was aware of Small's watching him as he went about his duties. After Spencer turned in for the evening, Wales attempted to pass through the officers' quarters to warn the first lieutenant, Mr. Gansevoort, but abandoned the plan when he saw that Spencer was still awake.

Wales lay awake all night and in the morning passed along his information to Purser Heiskill. The executive officer was alerted immediately, and Wales noticed that he was being watched closely by Boatswain's Mate Cromwell, Seaman Small, and two other sailors, Wilson and McKinley.

After learning of the alleged plot, Lieutenant Gansevoort went directly to Commander Mackenzie. Mackenzie said that he doubted a mutiny was afoot but ordered Gansevoort to keep a close watch on Spencer. Gansevoort was a seasoned officer with eighteen years' experience in the Navy. Though he saw no illicit action on Spencer's part, his intuition convinced him that the midshipman was up to no good.

Lieutenant Gansevoort also observed Spencer studying charts of the Isle of Pines—the first destination of the pirate ship *Somers*, according to Wales. Finding himself under the watchful eye of the first lieutenant, Spencer returned the look with "the most infernal expression I have ever seen upon a human face," Gansevoort testified later.

Commander Mackenzie conferred with Lieutenant Gansevoort and asked what course of action the latter recommended. The executive officer urged that Spencer be placed in irons on the quarterdeck immediately to prevent any further mutinous action on his part. The captain agreed.

Mackenzie approached Spencer and, according to his written reports, said, "I learn, Mr. Spencer, that you aspire to the command of the *Somers*?" The midshipman answered negatively, and the captain confronted him with Wales's allegations regarding the mutiny.

"I may have told him so, sir, but it was in joke," Spencer replied.

Commander Mackenzie ordered Spencer to remove his neckerchief, which Wales had mentioned contained a list of sailors loyal to the midshipman. While no such paper was found, Spencer was placed in irons. A search of the midshipman's belongings found two lists, both spelled in Greek letters. The first was a list of about thirty crew members divided into three categories: "Certain," "Doubtful," and "To be kept *nolens volens*, Latin for "willing or unwilling." The second paper listed duties for the reduced crew. Only four names were on the "Certain" list, including that of Midshipman Spencer.

The officer of the deck was now armed with a cutlass and pistol, and security was heightened. Officers were instructed to increase rounds during the night to prevent any violence.

The next day was Sunday, November 27, and Commander Mackenzie studied every face on board, first during inspection and then during the worship service. Two people bothered him greatly, and they were Spencer's closest allies—Boatswain's Mate Cromwell and Seaman Small.

Emotions were running high aboard the *Somers*. When a main-royal mast was carried away, a fairly common event, both Mackenzie and Gansevoort believed that it was an intentional act of sabotage. Shortly afterward, as the main-top-gallant mast was about to be swayed from the deck, a large group of sailors came running toward the captain and his first officer.

Gansevoort drew his Colt pistol and shouted that he would "blow the first man's brains out who should put his foot on the quarterdeck." Midshipman Henry Rodgers hurried aft to explain that he had simply ordered the crew to man the mast rope.

Later in the day, Commander Mackenzie ordered Gansevoort to arrest Cromwell and place him in irons on the suspicion of plotting a mutiny. Upon being questioned by the captain, Cromwell professed his innocence and claimed that Seaman Small was the guilty party. Small was then questioned by the captain. He did not dispute that he had been party to the planning, and he was placed in irons with the other two would-be mutineers.

Mackenzie now took the precaution of arming all his officers with pistols and cutlasses. The next day two men received floggings for minor offenses. Afterward, Commander Mackenzie addressed the crew and told them of the intended mutiny, stressing that many of them were to have been killed by Spencer and his accomplices.

Another crewman was punished the following day, Tuesday. Mackenzie obviously felt that discipline was deteriorating on the ship. Following the punishment, the captain observed the crew gathering in little groups and talking in hushed tones.

On Wednesday, conditions were worse in the captain's opinion—he felt a malignancy spreading throughout the ship. The arrest of four more sailors did nothing to ease mounting tensions. His officers, he believed, were at the snapping point. Commander Mackenzie or Lieutenant Gansevoort had been on deck continually for four days. The time had come for action.

That day Commander Mackenzie wrote a letter to his four wardroom officers and the three oldest midshipmen, seeking their advice on how best to deal with the crisis. The officers called various witnesses and deliberated all day, adjourning that night only at the request of the captain. While the *Somers* plowed through the quiet waters of the Caribbean, Mackenzie spent another sleepless night as he took charge of the starboard watch. Gansevoort had the port watch.

The next morning the officers were again locked in deliberation, and at nine they delivered a message to Commander Mackenzie. It was their opinion that the prisoners were "guilty of a full and determined intention to commit a mutiny." Furthermore, they wrote, "We are convinced that it would be impossible to carry them to the United States, and that the safety of the public property, the lives of ourselves, . . . require that (giving them sufficient time to prepare) they should be put to death. . . ."

It is important to note that the officers wrote that this was their "opinion." They had no authority to condemn men to death. Only a true court-martial could have sealed such a fate for convicted mutineers.

Nonetheless, Commander Mackenzie immediately set about making arrangements for the execution of Spencer, Cromwell, and Small, reasoning that, of the seven prisoners, they were the only ones who could navigate and direct the operation of the ship. By getting rid of the three alleged ringleaders, Mackenzie believed that he could prevent any more mutinous behavior.

Spencer and two other suspected ringleaders were hanged at sea, December, 1, 1842.

The three were to be hanged within two hours. According to Mackenzie's report, Spencer begged for mercy before regaining his composure. Cromwell denied his guilt to the last. Small admitted his guilt, warned his shipmates to use his death as an example in their lives, and worried about his mother.

In a macabre gesture, Mackenzie had Cromwell's head shaved after the execution to reveal the numerous scars he had earned by leading a villainous life. Midshipman Spencer's body was laid out in his dress uniform, minus his sword, and all three were buried at sea.

The rest of the journey to New York passed uneventfully, with Commander Mackenzie feeling once more in full command of his ship. It was only upon dropping anchor and going ashore that he began to lose control over his life.

The initial news reports of the *Somers* affair painted Commander Mackenzie as a hero who had quelled a vicious mutiny and who was justified in the extraordinary hanging of the three ringleaders, including the son of the secretary of war.

The New York newspapers of the day related grossly inaccurate accounts of a mutiny that never came to fruition. The *Herald* reported, "A midshipman aboard had led fifty of the crew in mutiny. . . ." According to the *Tribune*, "*Passed Midshipman SPENCER, son of John C. Spencer, our Secretary of War, the Boatswain's Mate, and the Master of Arms immediately led the way*, and were followed by thirteen apprentices and about sixty of the crew." The *New York Express* declared that Spencer had held a pistol to Mackenzie's chest, and that after a struggle, the officers overpowered the mutineers.

Mackenzie, for his part, kept quiet about the events, pending instructions from the Navy. He had sent his nephew and clerk, young Oliver Perry, to Washington with his official report, and he had briefed only his brother-in-law, Matthew C. Perry, commandant of the New York Navy Yard and Commodore Jacob Jones, commandant of the New York Naval Station.

Five days after the arrival of the *Somers* in port, the *Courier and Enquirer* ran a detailed article about the so-called mutiny that accurately followed Mackenzie's official report and praised the officer for his actions. Almost immediately dissenting opinions appeared in print. The *Herald*, which had offered kind words for Mackenzie just a few days earlier, pointed out that no mutinous act actually had been committed on board and that the three men executed had been killed without the benefit of a court-martial. The newspaper also reported the fact that one of the executed, Boatswain's Mate Samuel Cromwell, had professed his innocence to the end.

Two days later an anonymous letter appeared in the Washington newspaper *Madisonian*. Though it was signed only "S," few people thought the letter's author was anyone other than Secretary Spencer. Referring to the executions as "the bloody deed," the letter noted that after Midshipman Spencer, Boatswain's Mate Cromwell, and Seaman Elisha Small were placed in double irons, "no disorder of a mutinous character appeared" on board the *Somers*.

The letter also pointed out that the officers of the *Somers* did not examine witnesses in the presence of the prisoners, thus precluding any cross-examination and denying the prisoners the chance to defend themselves during testimony. The hearing held by the officers carried no weight, the letter maintained, since it was not a true court-martial and no oath had been invoked.

Perhaps most damning, the anonymous letter remarked that the three were executed "when every thing and person on board the vessel were perfectly quiet, after four days of entire security. . . ."

Despite the fact that George Upshur, a naval officer and brother of Secretary of the Navy Abel P. Upshur, was Mackenzie's closest professional friend, the secretary ordered a court of inquiry to investigate the alleged mutinous plot and subsequent executions. The court, made up of three naval officers and a judge advocate (who was a former naval officer and the current U.S. District Attorney for the Southern District of New York), wasted no time in assembling. The first day of the hearing was held on board the *U.S.S. North Carolina* on December 28, 1842, exactly one week after the *Somers*'s arrival in New York harbor.

The hearing, which lasted until January 20, drew a large attendance each day it was in session. Among those who took in the proceedings were maritime attorney Richard Henry Dana, Jr., author of the autobiographical *Two Years Before the Mast*, and James

Commander Alexander Slidell Mackenzie, seen here sketched at his court-martial, was found "not proven" of the charges against him.

Fenimore Cooper. Dana, always the champion of the common sailor, nevertheless came away from the court convinced that Mackenzie was an honorable man who had done the right thing. Cooper, a one–time friend of Mackenzie's, drew a different conclusion.

Because her husband had professed his innocence and repeatedly had been proclaimed innocent by Midshipman Spencer, Cromwell's widow filed an appeal to have Mackenzie tried in a civil court of law on the charge of murder. To sidestep a civilian trial, the commander requested a full court-martial before his first hearing was over.

The court of inquiry returned its decision January 28—ironically the day that Philip Spencer would have been nineteen. Commander Mackenzie was exonerated completely by the board.

The court-marital was convened February 1, 1843, with Commander Alexander Slidell Mackenzie charged with murder, oppression, illegal punishment, conduct unbecoming an officer, and cruelty. During the trial the charges of unnecessary cruelty and conduct unbecoming an officer were dropped.

Mackenzie's defense hinged on, first, proving the existence of the plot and, second, proving that he took the only course of action available to him. The first point was the easier of the two to establish. Mackenzie had the testimony of Purser's Steward Wales, which claimed that Midshipman Spencer had approached Wales in an effort to recruit him for the mutiny.

There was also the physical evidence of Spencer's two lists, made out in Greek letters, which included the names of those allegedly loyal to him and ascribing their duties. That only four names, including those of Spencer and Wales, were described as "Certain," and several other names could not be identified as actual members of the crew, was brushed aside.

The second point was more difficult and equally critical for Mackenzie. It was argued that the size of the brig and the small number of officers made the *Somers* vulnerable. Mackenzie also claimed that the "ominous looks" of the crew made him fearful of some sort of attempt to liberate Spencer and the others. The captain also dismissed the idea that he could have put in at St. Thomas or another foreign port to ask for help. Finally, Commander Mackenzie maintained that his officers were suffering from the strain of constantly being on watch, armed day and night.

The case was covered in detail in newspapers, including verbatim transcripts of the testimony. Mackenzie continued to have both supporters and detractors throughout the court-martial. Dana continued to write in strong support of Mackenzie. James Fenimore Cooper would wait until the trial was over before publishing a long invective of the *Somers*'s commanding officer. Mackenzie's old friend, Longfellow, wrote letters of encouragement, but Washington Irving was surprisingly quiet about the whole affair.

The strain of the trial began to affect Mackenzie's health. He fell ill, and the proceedings were postponed for several days. By then the court-martial had dragged on for a month and a half, and the public was beginning to lose interest. When the U.S. Circuit Court handed down its decision that Mackenzie could not be tried in a civil court, there ensued a flurry of activity to complete the court-martial.

On March 22 Mackenzie's defense counsel made his summation, painting a picture of what might have happened if Spencer, Cromwell, and Small had not been hanged but had been rescued by other would-be mutineers. What could have followed would have been the murder of the loyal crewmen and officers and the first instance of a U.S. warship turned pirate. If the court found Commander Mackenzie guilty, the defense concluded, it would "be the signal for the general prevalence of insubordination in our navy."

On March 27 another of the *Somers*'s officers, Passed Assistant Surgeon Richard Leecock, twenty-eight, shot and killed himself on board the *Somers* the night before Mackenzie's verdict was handed down. The next day, the court announced that it found Commander Mackenzie "not proven" of the charges. On the charge of murder, nine of the jury had voted not guilty, three voted guilty. Regarding the charge of illegal punishment, the jury had split eight to four. This was not an honorable acquittal but an acquittal all the same.

To everyone's surprise, Mackenzie made no move to press charges against the sailors he had ordered imprisoned as potential mutineers. When no charges were filed, the dozen men who had been held since early December were released. Many observers interpreted this as an acknowledgment that there had never been any real conspiracy to commit mutiny.

Commander Mackenzie was a free man, and he received the thanks of merchants in Boston, New York, and Baltimore, and Philadelphia, including signed petitions, assistance with his legal fees, and other handsome gifts. He was a broken man, however. His health never fully recovered, and he was not to have another command until four years later when he served briefly as captain of the *U.S.S. Mississippi*. Mackenzie died of a heart attack the following year, 1848, at the age of forty-five.

The *Somers* herself died a violent death. Under the command of Lieutenant Raphael Semmes (who would go on to earn glory as captain of the Confederate raider *C.S.S. Alabama)* the *Somers* heeled over in a squall off the coast of Mexico, quickly sinking on December 8, 1846. Thirty-two of the seventy-six officers and crew were lost and seven were captured by Mexican forces.

As an experimental school ship for naval apprentices, the *Somers* had proven to be a failure. Subsequently, the new secretary of the Navy, George Bancroft, was determined to create a permanent training ground for the Navy similar to that of the Army at West Point. In 1845, the opening of the U.S. Naval Academy at Annapolis ensured a new breed of professional officer for the service.

Literature also benefited from the would-be mutiny on the *Somers*. Although Mackenzie never got around to setting down the story on paper, nor his friend Longfellow create a poem about the affair as Mackenzie had hoped, another writer connected with the case made memorable use of the events. First officer Guert Gansevoort's cousin was Herman Melville.

Melville made a name for himself shortly after the *Somers* incident with the publication of *Typee* and went on to write some of the greatest masterpieces of American literature. But it was not until nearly fifty years later, after his death, that the novel that would eventually be considered second only to *Moby Dick* was published: *Billy Budd*, the story of cruelty aboard a warship and the hanging of a good sailor by a reluctant officer.

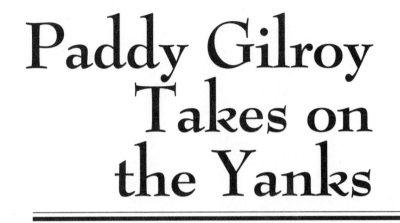

Paddy Gilroy Takes on the Yanks

IN THE NINETEENTH CENTURY, the undisputed masters of the sea were the whalers that sailed across the globe from the stony ports Down East. Hailing from such harbors as New Bedford, Stonington, Gloucester, and Nantucket, the whalemen and their hardy ships endured rigorous existences to track down and slay the leviathans of the deep.

The New England whalemen had surpassed the prowess and stamina of all others who attempted the dangerous but highly profitable trade of whaling, but the Yankees had never been very successful in one fertile whaling ground—the waters off Foveaux Strait, on the southwestern tip of New Zealand.

The seas there were abundant with whales, but they also were known to conjure merciless storms without much warning—howling tempests that would batter an unsuspecting crew and vessel as if they were children's toys.

At least one man was making huge profits taking whales off New Zealand; his name was Paddy Gilroy. The skill and daring of the native New Zealander was known up and down the eastern seaboard, but what interested the Yankee whalemen was the potential wealth in the waters of the Antipodes. It rankled them to think that Paddy Gilroy was the only man taking advantage of the situation.

One whaleman in particular, Captain Barnabus Briggs of New Bedford, was determined to make a profitable sailing to New Zealand and give Paddy Gilroy a run for his money. In the spring of 1878, Captain Briggs, skipper of the *Tamerlane*, led a fleet of five whalers out of New Bedford and headed for the South Pacific.

Some three months later, the Yankee whaling fleet, consisting of the *Tamerlane*, *Eliza Adams*, *Coral*, *Matilda Sears*, and the *Rainbow*, arrived at New Zealand. The captains and crews had been well warned of the unpredictable weather and felt themselves prepared to deal with whatever nature handed them.

It was Captain Briggs's argument that if Paddy Gilroy could make a fortune hunting whales, then surely the renowned whalemen from Down East could do the same.

As they neared the ominous cliffs of Foveaux Strait, the Yankees were treated to a strange sight: a dilapidated old windjammer named the *Chance*, bearing down on the *Tamerlane*.

Captain Briggs took out his eyeglass and studied the loose lines of the approaching ship. So, this was the vessel that had taken so many whales for the famed Paddy Gilroy! As he looked, Briggs could make out the figure of Gilroy himself. The man whom Captain Briggs had come to better was slouched against the *Chance*'s taffrail, his red hair covered by a most unseamanlike derby. He wore old canvas pants that were apparently made from sails that had seen better days. A tattered frock coat added a touch of decayed elegance to the appearance of the Kiwi captain.

Once Briggs had studied his adversary, he began to feel better about his mission. And Gilroy had achieved his purpose; he had been seen by the Americans and dismissed as some sort of lunatic. He had also lulled the Americans into a false sense of security. No one knew better than he how terrible the weather was in the whaling grounds; no one knew better how to deal with it.

The next morning, Captain Briggs was ready to get a head start. As the sun crept up past the horizon, the stalwart New Englander must have felt his pulse quicken as he looked across the water and saw

The Kiwi whalemen cutting in a whale.

literally thousands of whales cavorting in the calm seas. His joy quickly turned to dismay when he sighted Gilroy's *Chance* in the thick of the monsters, his whalemen already towing a prize bull whale.

Unknown to the American fleet, Gilroy had posted lookouts at the mastheads at midnight instead of dawn. The great herd of whales had lit up the seas by churning acres of phosphorescence and had been sighted quickly by the New Zealanders.

So the locals had scored the first victory; it couldn't be helped. Briggs decided to make the best of it, and boats were lowered from all five Yankee whalers. The whalemen rowed into the midst of the whales and made fast their harpoons. As was the custom, some were given a "Nantucket sleigh ride," being pulled some distance by the dying whales; others nearly capsized. Some hit their marks with apparent ease, while others threw dart after dart.

The boats slowly began making their way back to the ships, towing the enormous carcasses behind, the men straining already tired muscles against the oars. On board the *Tamerlane*, Captain Briggs saw to the preparations to receive the whales. The bodies would be attached to either side of the vessel, and the flensing and "cutting in" operations would begin in which the whales would be stripped of their valuable blubber. The blubber would go into the try pots to be rendered into precious sperm oil—the oil that would light the homes and businesses back in America. The ivory would be collected and stored in the hold to be sold for buttons and various knick knacks.

In his preparations, Captain Briggs was merely carrying out the traditions of whaling captains everywhere, just as he had hundreds of times before, all over the world. His mistake was not paying any attention to what his adversary was doing.

Paddy Gilroy had sufficed with one whale. He and his crew attached the carcass to a towline and set sail for the safety of Foveaux Strait. Briggs and the others continued their operations. The whales taken by the crew of the *Tamerlane* were not lashed alongside until well after noon. Similar actions were taking place aboard the other vessels.

A breeze that had been blowing for some time began to freshen; it seemed harmless enough until Captain Briggs caught sight of an ugly-looking front on the horizon. The wind veered around from the northeast, placing the safety of Foveaux Strait to windward.

As the strengthening wind began to tear at the ships, Briggs ordered the boats to be hoisted. The added weight of the whales made it necessary to run before the wind to keep from rolling in the heavy seas. Instead of dissipating as the captain had anticipated, the weather continued to worsen. The Yankee fleet was being driven farther toward the tempest-tossed seas of the Antarctic. Finally, Briggs gave the order to cut loose the whales.

The storm blew for five days, battering the whalers with punishing wind and waves. When the calm arrived, the Yankees regrouped.

The *Eliza Adams* and the *Coral* had suffered more damage than could be repaired at sea, and both were taking water. They would have to drop out of the season's whaling expedition and limp into the nearest dry dock.

The three remaining whalers, the *Tamerlane*, *Matilda Sears*, and the *Rainbow*, sailed through Foveaux Strait to Port William, where Paddy Gilroy had been holed up, working calmly on his whale. The *Chance* had sailed out through the strait as the Americans came in.

The Yankees stayed in port while repairs were made to the three whalers. A couple of days later, the *Chance* came into port with two large sperm whales lashed to her sides. Her captain seemed to be in good humor and cheerfully waved his derby at the docked New Englanders.

Repairs were completed upon the *Tamerlane*, but the ship had to stay in port while another vicious storm came up. Paddy Gilroy went about the business of rendering his whales.

Then one morning the crews of the American ships awoke to find that Paddy Gilroy and the *Chance* had slipped out of the harbor during the night. In a fair rage, Captain Briggs ordered the three Yankee ships to get under way as quickly as possible. It seemed that the foxlike Gilroy had outsmarted them again. Briggs had determined to deep a closer eye on Gilroy—he would sail when the New Zealander sailed, take whales when he took whales, and head to port when Gilroy headed to port.

The whalers soon found plentiful whales, and the *Chance* was in the middle of the action. Two boats were lowered away from the *Tamerlane*. Briggs was taking no chances. Normally he would have lowered the full complement of four whaleboats, but he did not want to be caught off guard by the winds again.

A little after noon, the Yankee boats towed back their darted whales to the waiting ships. Briggs was keeping his eyes on the weather—the sky had begun to darken and the breeze freshen—and Paddy Gilroy. The *Chance* had already come about and had put on clouds of sail. Briggs responded by having the *Tamerlane* come about and put on sail. The ship responded sluggishly in the mounting seas, hampered as she was by the massive whales lashed alongside.

The Yankees suddenly found themselves in a tight situation. The three whalers were being driven toward the rocks of Stewart Island. They were far enough inside the mouth of Foveaux Strait that they could not turn back for the open sea, but not far enough in to reach safety and keep their whales, too.

The crews of the three Yankee whalers kept their eyes on the *Chance*, which still held fast to her whale. The New Zealand ship seemed to be drifting dangerously close to Stewart Island and its jagged rocks. And still, Paddy Gilroy did not tack. Captain Briggs lost faith in the Kiwi whaleman. The man must truly be mad; he was past the point where he could have saved himself. As the Yankees watched in horror, the white waters off Stewart licked at the *Chance*.

It was a somewhat distraught Barnabus Briggs who ordered the whales to be cut loose. The heavy drags gone, the American whalers now raced toward the safety of Port William and escaped the apparent fate of Paddy Gilroy.

The following day, as Captain Briggs wrote in his journal, a cry on deck brought him topside. There was the *Chance*, a whale in tow, making her way into port. The jaunty New Zealand captain raised his derby in salute to the disbelieving Yankees.

Later, Briggs learned how Gilroy had escaped death on the rocks of Stewart Island. One of the sailors from the *Chance* told the American skipper that once the New Zealand vessel had reached the foam and spray, Captain Gilroy had ordered the yards trimmed and handily sailed through a narrow pass into a sheltered inlet. The New Zealanders had set about rendering their whale at Stewart Island and later tracked down one of the whales cast off by the Americans.

In the time that the Yankee whalers had been in the waters off New Zealand, they had lost two ships and taken no whales. Paddy Gilroy, aboard his dowdy *Chance*, had taken five whales. He had proven his continued superiority in those rich but dangerous seas.

The next morning saw the crestfallen Americans set sail for kinder cruising grounds. The Yankee whalers may have been the best in the business everywhere else, but the waters of New Zealand definitely belonged to Paddy Gilroy.

The
Icebound
Voyage
of the *Fram*

W ITH THE FINANCIAL BACKING of king and country, the trim vessel *Fram* sailed from Christiana (latter-day Oslo) on June 24, 1893. On board were Dr. Fridtjof Nansen and a handpicked crew of twelve sailors and scientists. They sought to be the first men to conquer the North Pole. And they intended to reach the pole aboard the *Fram*.

Critics of the day hailed the project as foolhardy and the work of amateurs. The ship, they contended, would be crushed to pieces by the pack ice, and the crew would be lost. It had happened before. Only twelve years earlier, the U.S. ship *Jeannette* had been destroyed, trapped in the ice north of the New Siberian Islands while undertaking an Arctic expedition.

Interestingly, it was the wreck of the *Jeannette* that had sparked Nansen's imagination. Timbers from the ship and identifiable articles of clothing had been discovered on the southwest coast of Greenland, some 2,000 miles from where the ship had gone down and three years after the wreck, suggesting to Nansen the existence of a transpolar current. Similarly, a type of hunting weapon made only by Alaskan Eskimos had been found on the coast of Greenland near Godthaab. If wreckage and bits of wood could float across the Arctic Ocean (and possibly near the North Pole), why not an entire ship?

In 1888 Nansen and a group of five others became the first men to cross the forbidding, uncharted interior of Greenland, skiing more than 400 miles cross country. Upon his return to Norway, Nansen was received as a hero.

In February 1890, the twenty-eight-year-old Nansen announced his intention to travel by boat to the North Pole. Addressing a meeting of the Christiana Geographic Society, the scientist-explorer proposed building a ship that could withstand the tremendous pressure created by Arctic ice floes. The vessel would be purposely trapped in the ice, and the crew would wait for the transpolar current to carry the ship to or near the pole.

The expedition would take anywhere from two to five years, Nansen believed. While waiting to reach their destination, the explorers would make use of their time in the Arctic by conducting valuable research and experiments.

Detractors notwithstanding, the funds for the project were easily raised. The public provided more than one-third of the money, and the king himself donated 20,000 kroner, more than $5,300, for the expedition.

Dr. Nansen contacted noted Scottish shipwright Colin Archer, and the two designed a short (one hundred twenty-eight feet), broad (thirty-six feet), three-masted schooner fitted with an auxiliary steam engine. The hull of the ship measured from twenty-four-to-twenty-eight inches thick. The sides were rounded and smooth to prevent the ice from "grabbing" the vessel. As Nansen wrote, "The object was that the whole craft should be able to slip like an eel out of the embrace of the ice." The hull was reinforced to resist the pressure of the ice, and extra insulation of reindeer hair, cork, and other materials was installed to keep the men comfortable during their long voyage.

Nansen's wife, Eve, christened the vessel *Fram*, Norwegian for "forward," on October 26, 1892. For the next nine months Nansen busied himself outfitting the ship, selecting his crew, and making

The Fram *sailed from Norway bound for the Arctic in the summer of 1893.*

final preparations for the expedition. Captain of the *Fram* would be Otto Sverdrup, who had accompanied Nansen on his Greenland expedition.

The ship sailed from Christiana to the Samoyed village of Khabarova, where thirty-four huskies were taken aboard, a gift from Russian explorer Baron Eduard von Toll. Von Toll had also deposited caches of food in the New Siberian Islands in the event that the crew of the *Fram* needed them.

Within three months of her June 1893 departure, the *Fram* found herself firmly encased in the Arctic ice. The ship's rudder was removed, the engine taken apart and placed in storage, and a windmill set up to supply energy for the *Fram*'s generator. Now it was simply a matter of waiting.

They didn't have to wait long for a test of the ship's strength. On

October 9, two weeks after becoming lodged in the ice, a "deafening noise" exploded around the ship. The pack ice had begun squeezing the *Fram*. All hands ran up on deck to witness the spectacle. It was the moment of truth. Terrific rumblings filled the air, and the ice shook as if from an earthquake. Magnificently, the *Fram* rose up from the ice. When the pressure lessened, she lowered herself again. Just as Nansen had hoped, the ship had slipped away from the ice's deadly grip.

The crew had begun gathering its scientific data. Meteorological readings were made every four hours. Astronomical observations were made every other day to track the *Fram*'s course. Humidity and temperature were checked. Soundings were made to determine the depth of the Arctic ocean, and the salinity and temperature of the water were also recorded regularly.

Nansen placed himself in charge of studying the Northern Lights. A scientist with the soul of a poet, Nansen wrote of the aurora borealis, "This is the coming earth—here are beauty and death. But to what purpose? Ah, what is the purpose of all these spheres? Read the answer, if you can, in the starry blue firmament."

The crew also had time for recreation. Bear hunts, walks along the ice, and animated conversations helped while away idle time. Card games, singing, and reading were also popular pastimes. The ship's doctor even started a newspaper, the *Fram Sjaa*.

Nansen had made sure that provisions were diverse enough to prevent boredom. The men dined on hard bread, cheese, corned beef, corned mutton, ham, tongue, bacon, cod roe, anchovies, oatmeal biscuits, potatoes, green vegetables, macaroni, orange marmalade, jelly, tea, coffee, and chocolate.

And so life continued. Thirteen men in an ice cube, hoping to conquer passively a goal that had frustrated explorers and adventurers in its mystic unattainability. The *Fram* drifted northwest, slowly, then veered toward the south before taking up her northern trek again. Nansen began to think that the voyage might take as long as eight years.

The winter passed. In April, the crew witnessed a solar eclipse;

summer brought the discovery of previously unknown bacteria by microscope. In August 1894 Nansen confidently predicted that the *Fram* would be home in two years, but he had secretly begun planning an overland passage to the pole.

Nansen was a man of action, and the inactivity of shipboard life disagreed with him. In his journal, he wrote, "This carefree life, this passive existence oppresses me. Ah! The very soul freezes. What would I not give for a single day of struggle—for even a moment of danger!"

Nansen told Captain Sverdrup of his plan to attain the North Pole by dogsled. As his partner he chose Hjalmar Johansen, a lieutenant in the Norwegian Naval Reserve. The two moved out of the *Fram* and began testing various cold weather gear to determine what would be best to take with them.

On March 14, 1895, the two set off with three sleds, twenty-seven dogs, and two kayaks. The *Fram* lay only 350 miles from the pole. Yet the two men would not be able to return to their ship as she continued her westward drift.

The going proved easy at first. Nansen and Johansen rigged sails on their sleds and flew across the smooth ice, but soon ridges and hummocks slowed their progress. By April 6, the two had reached 86° 2.8′ N and were within 272 miles of the pole. Nansen, however, knew that their time was running short. The floes they were on were drifting south almost as fast as Nansen and Johansen could travel north. If rough terrain continued to slow their progress, the two explorers would be forced to turn back and race for land.

They struggled northward for three more days before deciding to turn back. They had reached 86° 14′ N and were within 224 miles of their goal—the two had traveled 160 miles closer to the North Pole than anyone before. Now the race was on to reach Franz Josef Land, a group of islands 400 miles to the south.

The journey south would turn out to be the most difficult part of the expedition. The Arctic spring and early summer presented many hazards to the adventurers. Ice turned to knee-deep slush that slowed progress. Miles of ice too thin to support the sleds but too thick for the kayaks forced the Norwegians to make long, arduous detours.

The dogs were running low on food and were visibly weakening. The only solution was, as Nansen described it, "a horrible affair." The weaker dogs were killed one by one to feed the stronger dogs. The team pushed southward. By the middle of June, only three dogs remained. Nansen and Johansen worked side by side with the dogs, pulling the sleds.

Finally, on July 24, the men spotted land, but it took them two weeks to reach the open water surrounding the island. With great sadness, the two men killed their two remaining dogs before putting their kayaks in the water. They explored the islands for three weeks before deciding to build winter quarters.

The two erected a small stone hut and roofed it with walrus hides. During the winter they dined on the same thing almost every day: bear meat soup for breakfast and fried bear steak for dinner. They slept on bearskins for as much as twenty hours a day and used bear fat in the stove and lamps. They talked about food, soft clothes, and hot baths and soap: "What a magnificent invention soap really is," Nansen wrote.

On May 19, 1896 the two started southward again. On June 17, Nansen went for a walk while Johansen cooked breakfast. Incredibly, Nansen heard a dog bark. Then he saw a man approaching and recognized him as English explorer Frederick Jackson. Jackson seized Nansen by the hand and said, "By Jove, I am glad to see you!"

Nansen and Johansen stayed in Jackson's well-stocked hut until the supply ship *Westward* arrived and gave them passage back to Norway. Shortly after his triumphant return, Nansen received a telegram that read, "Fridtjof Nansen: Fram arrived in good condition. All well on board. Shall start at once for Tromso. Welcome home. Otto Sverdrup." The good ship had drifted westward and southward, freeing herself of the pack ice near Spitsbergen. She had gone farther north than any other ship before her, reaching 85° 57′ N in October 1895. She had proven Nansen's theory about transpo-

Despite his failed attempt to reach the Pole, Dr. Fridtjof Nansen was a most remarkable man.

lar currents, and she had come through unscathed, with all hands on board.

The *Fram* was to see more action when fellow Norwegian Roald Amundsen borrowed the ship from Nansen and became the first man to reach the South Pole on December 14, 1911. The ship can be seen today at the Fram Museum in Oslo.

Nansen soon found himself serving as a statesman and was largely responsible for securing Norway's independence from Sweden through diplomatic talks. He was called upon by the League of Nations to effect the repatriation of more than 400,000 prisoners of war held in Russia before turning his efforts to repatriating Turks and Greeks. Over the years Dr. Nansen continued his humanitarian efforts and, in 1922, was awarded the Nobel Prize for Peace.

His accomplishments were many: scientist, professor, inventor, author, adventurer, explorer, diplomat. But Fridtjof Nansen's polar expedition remained his crowning achievement—described as nothing less than "the greatest human exploit of the nineteenth century."

A Decade of Splendor, Speed, and Sail

T HE MAXIM "Time is money" has been true for as long as man has conducted business, and during no other era did man attempt to conquer time in a more beautiful or graceful way than he did in the brief age of the clipper ship.

The history for the quest for speed at sea is lengthy, in America dating back at least to pre-Revolutionary smugglers. Speed, in fact, became necessary for the very survival of men at sea, both merchants and warriors.

The clipper ship, as such, was not an overnight development. The word *clipper* comes from the Icelandic "to cut," and to sailors, originally it only denoted the idea of speed. Therefore, any fast model hull that was quick was considered a clipper, regardless of rig.

The reasons for the development of American clipper ships were three-fold: the expansion of the China tea trade, the California Gold Rush, and the repeal of the British Navigation Acts. New tea-exporting ports were opened in China in 1842; the Gold Rush broke in 1849. Suddenly American shippers were allowed to compete with British shippers sailing into British ports. The necessity for speed in all three cases is obvious. Tea spoiled quickly at sea; prospectors wanted to get to California as fast as possible; and the fastest merchant ships would get the most trade.

Scholars argue as to who built the first true clipper ship; that is, who developed the first three-masted vessel that was square-rigged all around. Apparently, two such ships were developed at about the same time. One of them was designed by Nat Palmer, the veteran sailor who as a youth had discovered the continent of Antarctica during a sealing expedition.

Palmer left sealing and began sailing for Edward Knight Collins, owner of the Louisiana Line. Palmer was dedicated to sailing faster than anyone else, and he was quite successful with Collins's flat-floored packets.

Late in the 1830s, Palmer designed a series of packets for Collins's transatlantic Dramatic Line. The result was a fleet of ships that could outsail the best of the American ships of the line.

Palmer turned next to the China trade. After learning the nature of the Chinese monsoons, the ambitious Yankee sailor began toying with a design for a new type of ship. He whittled a model and showed it to William Low of A.A. Low and Brothers of New York. The ship was agreed upon, and in 1844 the finished product, the *Houqua*—named for a venerable Chinese merchant—was launched. She sailed from New York to Hong Kong in a record-setting eighty-four days. It was the beginning of a new era for ships and shippers.

At the same time, naval architect John Willis Griffiths was busy designing a fast ship of his own. Griffiths radically changed the traditional bluff bow to a flared bow, "turning them inside out," as waterfront observers of the day claimed. Griffiths also had to reposition the foremast farther aft. The concave shape of the waterline near the stern was also done away with.

The result of this scientific redesigning was the *Rainbow*, launched in New York in 1845. The *Rainbow* is considered by many to be the first true clipper, although she was consistently slower than the *Houqua*.

It was not until Griffiths built his second clipper, the *Sea Witch*, that the clipper design was perfected. The *Sea Witch* was a thoroughbred clipper, with hollow water lines and clouds of sail above.

With the advent of the Gold Rush in California, clipper followed

Donald McKay's clipper Flying Cloud *could sail 374 miles a day.*

clipper to meet the demand of fortune seekers. The *Sovereign of the Seas* sailed from New York to San Francisco in 103 days, despite being dismasted and rerigged en route. Donald McKay, who became the nation's foremost clipper builder, launched the famous *Flying Cloud* in 1851. This extreme clipper was designed, unabashedly, for all-out speed, and she could cover some 374 miles in a single day.

Between 1851 and 1853, the *Ino* regularly sailed from Singapore to New York in only eighty-six days. The *Pilot* could raise Salem ninety-six days out of Manila. The world of international trade was on its ear, with each company and every captain trying to outdo the other in terms of speed. So confident of his ship's speed was the famous Captain Samuels that, if his *Dreadnought* did not deliver her freight in a certain time period, he would refuse payment.

By 1855, just a short decade after the appearance of the revolutionary clipper, its popularity began to wane. More than 120 clippers were launched in 1853, but 1855 saw only 42 of the great vessels come off the ways. None of them were the ships of daring design like the *Flying Cloud*. Only three clippers were launched in 1859.

The reasons for the demise of the clippers were several. The Gold Rush had tapered off; 1857 saw a freight depression; and a new type of vessel was beginning to ply the trade routes in growing numbers—the steamship.

The *Savannah*, the first steamer to cross the Atlantic, had made her trailblazing passage in 1819, and the Cunard Line had steamers crossing from New York to Liverpool in fewer than eleven days before 1850. In April of that year, the American Collins Steamship Line began business. The Collins steamships were faster than the Cunarders, but because faster ships burned more fuel and were therefore less economical than slower vessels, the Collins Line was short-lived. The future of shipping was clear, however. It belonged to steamships.

American shipbuilders still built a few clippers, almost exclusively for British shippers, but their days of glory and speed were over.

One of the last great clippers built was the famous *Cutty Sark*, launched in November 1869. Despite modernizations and her immense sail area, the English clipper never lived up to expectations. She was continually slower than her rival, the *Thermopylae*, built a year earlier. The *Cutty Sark* sailed in the tea trade until 1877, but the steamships were too competitive in the China trade, helped in large part by the opening of the Suez Canal.

The *Cutty Sark* went the way of many of the old-time clippers. She hauled odd cargoes, sailed in the Australian wool trade, was sold to the Portuguese, and finally was rerigged as a barkentine. What had once been a lavish lady became little more than a dowdy tramp.

The clipper era has been cited as "the most remarkable ten years of sail in the history of the world." And indeed it was. The seagoing world had seen the future, though, and the future belonged to steam.

The Wireless Proves Itself

I T WAS JANUARY 22, 1909, and a raw winter night in New York City as the White Star Line's *Republic* nosed her way down the Hudson River. She carried 460 winter-weary passengers seeking the warmer climes of the Mediterranean.

At his post on the bridge, Captain William Sealby was in good humor. The *Republic* was a fine vessel, only five years old. At 570 feet long, the ocean-liner was one of the newest and fastest passenger ships afloat, and she featured a fairly new communications development—the wireless radio.

As the liner passed through the Ambrose Channel toward the lightship, the air began to thicken with mist. The officers and men on the bridge were not overly concerned; a little fog was pretty usual stuff for this time of year. Below, the passengers were lingering over cocktails or enjoying last smokes before turning in for the night.

At the Ambrose Lightship, Sealby gave the order to his helmsman to follow a northerly course toward the Nantucket sea buoy. At that point the *Republic* would turn east and begin her run across the Atlantic. Meanwhile, the fog began to grow heavier.

In pre-radar and sonar days, visibility played a far more important role than it does for mariners now. The *Republic* was steaming in heavily traveled waters. Not only did the vessel run the risk of straying off course, but the danger of close-range encounters with other ships loomed. As the fog closed in on the luxury ship, Captain Sealby ordered lookouts to be posted at stem and stern, and slowed the vessel to half speed.

The captain also ordered the ship's foghorn to be activated: a six-second blast every minute. The *Republic* inched her way across the water, moving cautiously northeast. The fog had made it impossible to sight any landmarks or take a star sighting; nevertheless, the ship's navigator continued to plot a course on his chart, using the vessel's speed and number of engine revolutions in his estimates.

Captain Sealby now had his ship on an easterly heading. According to the navigator, the *Republic* lay some thirty miles southwest of Nantucket. It was 5:30 on the morning of January 23, and the fog enshrouded them as thickly as ever.

Suddenly, someone on the bridge cried out that he thought he saw something. Sealby immediately ordered all engines stopped. The lookouts and those on watch peered intensely into the fog on the ship's port side. As they looked, to their horror, a shadowy figure emerged from the mist.

The order, "Full speed astern," was given, followed quickly by, "left full rudder." The *Republic*'s foghorn sounded three times in quick succession. Sealby was attempting to scoot his 570 feet of steel out of harm's way.

Lights broke through the fog on the port side. Not just green, not just red, but red, green, and white, meaning another ship was bearing down directly upon the *Republic*. Sealby reversed the engines to full speed ahead, and the liner shuddered under the strain.

It was too late. The bow of the second vessel plowed into the *Republic*, instantly killing two passengers as they slept in their staterooms. Captain Sealby swung into action, stopping the engines and calling for damage reports.

The startled passengers were ordered up on deck as stewards went to work getting food and coffee together. The communications man, a youth named Jack Binns, hurried to the radio shack to report the collision.

The Republic went down in January 1909, at the time the largest ship to sink in the Atlantic.

The *Republic* had taken a hard hit, and the damage was considerable. A large vertical gash had been ripped in the port side and ran below the waterline. The engine room had been penetrated and was taking water. Almost immediately, the vessel began to list to port.

A few thousand yards away lay the S.S. *Florida* of the Lloyd Italiano Line. Her bow was smashed, and the captain and his passengers were shaken. Captain Angelo Ruspini, only twenty-nine years old, had heard the *Republic*'s foghorn too late. He had reduced speed and sounded his own foghorn, but to no avail. Seeing the liner appear from the fog, the Italian had reversed his engines but was unable to stop in time to avert the disaster. His entire bow section had caved in, and three members of the crew were killed in the forecastle.

On board the *Republic*, Binns, the radio man, worked steadily at his key. The ship's power had gone off, thanks to the water in the engine room, and Binns had switched over his set to battery power, severely limiting his broadcast range. He tapped out the maritime disaster signal "CQD," for "Come Quick Danger."

The *Florida* had no wireless set—it was still a relatively new invention and was considered expensive. Although the necessity of a ship's wireless had yet to be proven to the world, it was the only way the ships' predicament could be communicated to anyone able to help.

Binns continued to tap out the message until he received a reply at 6:15 A.M. A. H. Ginman, a wireless operator at the lifesaving station at Siasconset on Nantucket sent the reply, "What is the nature of your emergency?"

Binns explained that the ship had been rammed. When asked the vessel's position, Binns was unable to answer and sought out the captain who gave the following message to be relayed to the shore: "*Republic* rammed by unknown steamship, twenty-six miles southwest Nantucket, badly in need of assistance."

On board the *Florida*, Captain Ruspini was worried. He continued sounding his ship's foghorn but noticed that the ship he had rammed was no longer blowing her own. He realized that the other vessel could be seriously damaged, and his own situation looked bad. With more than thirty feet of bow caved in, the *Florida* was no longer stable in the water. Most of her passengers were Italian immigrants who had survived a terrible earthquake in Messina a few weeks earlier, and there was a growing panic aboard the ship.

On the beach at Siasconset, radio operator Ginman was busy sending the message to wireless operators of all ships at sea with his powerful set. The French ship *La Touraine* responded to the call and changed course. Another of the recipients of the distress call was the steamship *Baltic*, bound for New York out of Liverpool. Captain J. B. Ranson checked his position against that of the *Republic*. He figured the ships were about sixty-four miles apart, some three hours distant, steaming at top speed. The *Baltic* responded to the call for help at 7:15.

The Italian skipper brought the *Florida* alongside the crippled *Republic*. After identities were exchanged, Captain Sealby requested that the *Florida* take on the 459 passengers who crowded the decks of the *Republic*. Captain Ruspini agreed. Passengers began transferring to the Italian liner, women and children first. Two hours later, the transfer was complete.

In the meantime, Jack Binns had received a message from the *Baltic*. Captain Ranson reckoned that the ships were now no more than ten miles apart, but because of the dense fog, he was having difficulty locating the *Republic* and the *Florida*.

On board his ship, Captain Ruspini was having trouble with the passengers of the two liners. Those from the *Republic* were mostly tourists who expected first-class treatment, and the immigrants aboard the *Florida* felt somewhat intimidated. A few fights broke out, but the officers and crew were able to keep problems to a minimum.

Captain Sealby ordered his men to fire rockets to signal his position to the *Baltic*, but Captain Ranson and his crew were unable to hear or see the rockets. The only contact depended upon the radio operators. The search continued.

The *Republic* had taken on a considerable amount of water. The engine room was the largest compartment on the liner and was now filled with water. Despite getting the passengers off, the vessel was still in danger of sinking. More than twelve hours had passed since the ramming, and the *Republic*'s stern was riding low in the water.

A rocket was heard to the northeast of the *Republic*. Captain Sealby had Binns radio the message: "Captain *Baltic*: there is a bomb bearing northeast from me. Keep firing."

The men strained to hear another rocket explosion. The minutes ticked by in silence. Then another explosion was heard. Relief swept through the ship's crew and officers, and Sealby ordered that the ship's bell be rung continuously to guide the approaching *Baltic*.

The *Florida* had begun to take water in her front hold, and Captain Ruspini decided to steam for New York. Radio messages flashed between *Baltic* and *Republic* as Captain Sealby sent instructions to his rescuers. The *Baltic* steamed into sight at last and maneuvered alongside the *Republic*.

The Italian ship had still not left for New York, her captain deciding instead to wait and try to alleviate his overcrowded decks. The three skippers held a conference and agreed that it would be best to transfer the passengers, some 1,650 in all, from the *Florida* to the *Baltic*. An hour before midnight, the tiring process of moving passengers by lifeboat began.

By ten the next morning, all the passengers had been relocated to the *Baltic*, which now steamed toward New York accompanied by the crippled *Florida*. Once the fog lifted, the *Republic* was taken under tow by the revenue cutter *Gresham*, the destroyer *Seneca*, and the S.S. *Furnessia*, one of several more merchant ships which had responded to the calls for assistance. Among the vessels now present were several liners, cutters, and freighters.

At 6:40 P.M., the stern line parted, releasing the *Republic* from the grip of the *Furnessia*. Later, the *Gresham* cut the bow line. Within two hours, the once magnificent *Republic* had sunk from view, the largest ship ever to sink in the Atlantic. Captain Sealby, First Officer Williams, and radio man Binns had been the last to abandon ship, climbing higher and higher until the doomed vessel slipped beneath the waves.

What had started out as a routine cruise to the Mediterranean had ended in disaster, with five people killed and one ship sunk. It could have been far worse, however, if it had not been for the level-headedness of Captain Sealby, the willingness of Captain Ranson to respond to the distress call, and Jack Binns's steady hand at the wireless radio—the instrument that brought them together.

The
Indomitable
Admiral
Benbow

ADMIRAL BENBOW. It is a name that, even if most people do not know its origin, is nonetheless familiar. Ballads record the deeds of the courageous officer, and Robert Louis Stevenson immortalized the name in *Treasure Island*, citing what may have been the first Admiral Benbow Inn.

Born in 1653, John Benbow was the son of a Shrewsbury tanner. Having served in the merchant marine from a tender age, Benbow joined the British Navy as a master's mate when he was twenty-five.

Under the tutelage of the rough Captain Philip Herbert, later Earl of Torrington, Benbow distinguished himself in actions against Mediterranean pirates.

For a brief time Benbow returned to the merchant marine. It was during this period that the seaman-turned-officer began to make a name for himself. His ship, aptly named the *Benbow*, found herself beset by pirates. The crew proved themselves to be stalwart fighters, and once the melee had subsided, no fewer than thirteen pirates' corpses adorned the bloody decks of the *Benbow*. At that time in Spain it was common for a bounty to be paid for pirates' heads.

Accordingly, Benbow had the bodies decapitated and the heads preserved in a vat of pork pickle.

As Benbow and his servant Caesar were leaving the *Benbow* in Cadiz, port officials demanded to see what the captain carried in his bulky burlap bag. Benbow made a great show of indignation, protesting that a captain as well known as himself should be above suspicion.

The customs officers apologized but insisted that the contents of the bag be made known. The captain agreed to present his case to the local magistrates. It must have been with some amusement that Benbow went before the solemn judge. Maintaining that the bag contained nothing but salt provisions, he reluctantly yielded to their authority, adding that the magistrates could keep the provisions if they desired. The sack was opened, and out tumbled the thirteen pickled pirates' heads.

The judges were overcome with admiration for such a brave captain who could capture and kill so many barbarous pirates and heartily congratulated Benbow. Word of the merchant captain's valor reached the Spanish monarch, who summoned Benbow to court to tell his own story.

Soon afterward, Benbow was restored to the Navy and began his rapid advancement through the ranks. He was promoted from third lieutenant to captain within four months and was made Master of Chatham Dockyard. A few weeks later, he was made Master of the Fleet at the Battle of Beachy Head, serving under his old mentor, Admiral Philip Herbert.

The battle was disastrous for Herbert, but Benbow's reputation remained intact. In fact, Benbow was becoming something of a hero, in addition to being a favorite of the king. Everywhere, people spoke of "the famous Captain Benbow."

In 1692, Benbow served as Master of the Fleet at the Battle of La Hogue; the following year he commanded a squadron during the bombardment of St. Malo and spent much of his time chasing down Channel privateers.

In 1698, Benbow sailed for the West Indies, commanding a squadron charged with protecting British interests and hunting such

In 1692, Benbow served as Master of the Fleet at the Battle of La Hogue.

pirates as the infamous Captain Kidd. While in the area, Benbow, now a rear admiral, returned two vessels that had been taken from Scottish colonists by the Spanish.

Despite the admiral's popularity back home, there were those who resented this commoner who had risen to prominence so rapidly. And certainly, Benbow did little to earn the love of higher-born officers. Though his courage and valor were unquestionable, Benbow had never enjoyed outstanding success in his engagements. In the colonies Benbow infuriated officials by impressing crewmen, but, to his credit, the admiral was noted for his great concern for the common sailor.

In 1700, Benbow was ordered back to England but returned to the West Indies the following year as Vice Admiral of the Blue. Once in colonial waters, the admiral returned to his practice of impressing crewmen from among the colonists. Answering criticism from the Admiralty, Benbow cited necessity before law.

In August of 1702, Admiral Benbow and his squadron encountered four French vessels running for the port of Cartagena. Benbow ran up the signal for his squadron to form a line of battle.

Inexplicably, the other ships did not readily comply, and it took an incredible three hours for the squadron to assemble and attack the French fleet. The French, despite being led by the brilliant and courageous Admiral J. B. Ducasse, entertained little hope of emerging victorious from the battle. The British had seven ships to the French's four, three of which were merely troop transport ships.

After a few exchanges of broadsides, Benbow found that only his ship, *H.M.S. Breda*, and that of Captain Walton, *H.M.S. Ruby*, remained in the fight. The other British ships had all withdrawn to a safe distance. Orders to return to battle were ignored.

Admiral Benbow and Captain Walton kept up the attack until the following day when the *Ruby* was so badly damaged that she had to retire from the fight and limp into Jamaica. The other British ships lay by idly, as the frustrated but persistent admiral continued the battle alone.

On the fourth day of the engagement, the forty-eight gun *Falmouth* came to the aid of the *Breda*. Together, the British ships captured the French ship *Anne* and were on the verge of taking a second ship as night fell. In the meantime, Benbow was seriously wounded when a French cannonball struck his leg. To his humiliation, the admiral watched as the French vessels gathered around their wounded ship and towed it off to safety, unhampered by the waiting British men-of-war.

The admiral sent a message to each of his captains, imploring them to behave "like Englishmen." To his surprise, Captain Kirby of *H.M.S. Defiance* presented a paper to the admiral demanding that he break off the attack in the face of insurmountable odds. All of the captains had signed the document, including Captain Christopher Fogg of the *Breda* and Captain Samuell Vincent of the *Falmouth*.

Benbow had no choice but to quit the battle. The amazed French fleet fled to Cartagena, and the British squadron sailed for Jamaica, where the admiral's leg was amputated.

Several weeks later a court-martial was convened in which Captains Richard Kirby and Cooper Wade were tried for cowardice and other crimes. John Constable was charged with breach of orders and neglect of duty. Fogg and Vincent were charged with advocating the abandonment, even though they had performed their duties. Thomas Hudson, captain of the *Pendennis*, had in the meantime died of an illness. Walton, as captain of the *Ruby*, was not tried; he had fought bravely until his ship was disabled.

Kirby and Wade were found guilty and sentenced to death by firing squad. Constable was also found guilty and dismissed from the service. Fogg and Vincent were found guilty of signing the mutinous paper, but they maintained that they had signed because they feared acts of treachery from the others if they did not. The two went unpunished.

On April 16, 1703, Kirby and Wade were executed on board *H.M.S. Bristol* in Plymouth. Whether they had refused to fight out of cowardice or to ruin the admiral who had once been a common seaman has never been established.

Even though Admiral Benbow died from his wounds some weeks after the court-martial, his name was destined to live on in the minds of sailors, travelers, and readers the world over.

The
Ship that
Met Herself
in Battle

THE ELEVEN-YEAR-OLD Cunard liner *Carmania* was at sea when her skipper, Captain James Barr, learned that war had been declared between Great Britain and Germany. Because of his line's commitment to the British government, Captain Barr assumed, correctly, that his vessel would be turned over to the Admiralty upon her arrival in England. At age sixty, he also assumed, this time incorrectly, that that would put an end to his sea duties.

On August 6, 1914, Captain Noel Grant, Royal Navy, received orders to take command of the *Carmania* and convert her into an armed cruiser. She would be the largest vessel he had ever commanded—675 feet long, displacing 19,500 tons. Grant was further instructed to offer a commission to Captain Barr, giving him the rank of commander in the Royal Naval Reserve and retaining his services as navigator and adviser.

The *Carmania* arrived the next morning in Liverpool, where she was met by Captain Grant and his first officer, Lieutenant Commander Edmund Lockyer, R.N., who immediately set to work transforming the luxury liner into a ship of war. Her hull was painted black, and the trademark red and black Cunard funnel was replaced by the color scheme of ubiquitous military gray.

Royal Navy sailors riveted armor plating onto the liner's most vulnerable spots and mounted eight 4.7-inch-caliber guns with a designated range of 9,300 yards. Bulwarks were cut away fore and aft to allow the guns to be worked, and decks and passenger quarters were cleared of unnecessary clutter.

Captain Barr accepted his commission in the Naval Reserve—it not only meant that he would be employed at sea, but he would have the satisfaction of remaining with his ship. Captain Grant moved into Barr's former cabin, and the newly commissioned Commander Barr somewhat slyly shifted his belongings to the larger and more luxurious quarters normally reserved for directors of the Cunard line.

Across the Atlantic, the captain of the brand-new luxury liner *Cap Trafalgar*, the pride of the Hamburg-SudAmerika Line, had also learned of the outbreak of war and of plans to outfit his vessel as an armed cruiser. The ship was the line's flagship, the largest and most luxurious liner sailing the South Atlantic. She measured 613 feet long and displaced 18,805 tons—roughly the same size as the *Carmania*.

Unfortunately, Captain Fritz Langerhannsz did not enjoy the numerous advantages granted the *Carmania*. First, his ship lay in Buenos Aires, not in a German port. Second, the German Admiralty had ordered the ship's conversion under the mistaken belief that she had on board armament that could be mounted on preexisting gun rings. The only weapons on board were Captain Langerhannsz's pistol and a pair of presentation shotguns. And third, the *Cap Trafalgar* was low on coal.

To compound his problems, some 150 of *Kapitän* Langerhannsz's crew, including four officers, had departed to return to Germany as reservists or volunteers. *Korvettenkapitän* August Moller now informed Langerhannsz that, while the latter would retain command of the *Cap Trafalgar*, his first officer, *Kapitänleutnant* Berend Feddersen, would take command in times of military action.

The *Cap Trafalgar*'s first order of business was to take on more

The Cunard liner Carmania *would become the first passenger vessel to sink another in an act of war.*

coal, and she departed Buenos Aires for Montevideo to do just that. After loading 3,500 tons of coal, she was to report to Trinidad Island, a barren spit of land 650 nautical miles off the coast of Brazil.

Meanwhile, the *Carmania* had been ordered to patrol an area of the Irish Channel, with the understanding that she would soon be dispatched to Nova Scotia to take up patrol duty on that side of the Atlantic. While the *Cap Trafalgar* was taking on coal in Uruguay, however, the *Carmania* received new orders: proceed at once to Bermuda.

On board the still unarmed *Cap Trafalgar*, Langerhannsz decided to disguise his vessel in order to better protect her. The aftermost of the ship's three funnels was a dummy stack and served only as a ventilator for the passenger decks, the galleys, and the generators' exhaust. If the funnel could be dismantled, the *Cap Trafalgar* could be made to look like a British passenger ship.

One of the passengers on board, Dr. Hans Braunholz, a veterinarian, had sailed on a certain British liner and offered press clippings and photographs of that vessel. Captain Langerhannsz studied the photos and determined that his ship could be made to look like the British liner, the name of which was *Carmania*.

Langerhannsz's crew set to work dismantling the dummy stack. The remaining two funnels were painted red and black in the Cunard tradition. The captain requisitioned canvas backdrops from an opera company traveling aboard the ship and put the troupe's stage manager in charge of building dummy wings to make the ship's bridge resemble that of the *Carmania*.

The finishing touches, a British red ensign and the Cunard line flag, were sewn and readied for action. En route to Trinidad Island, the *Cap Trafalgar* had transformed herself into the *Carmania*. She reached the island on August 28.

The next day, the real *Carmania* steamed from Bermuda for the West Indies where she was to join Admiral Sir Christopher Cradock's squadron in patrolling the coastal waters and river mouths along Venezuela, searching for the German cruisers *S.M.S. Dresden* and *S.M.S. Karlsruhe*.

The British Admiralty had intercepted numerous encoded German radio transmissions that led them to believe that Trinidad Island might be a rendezvous point for German vessels. On September 11, the *Carmania* received orders to search the Vas Rocks and the waters around Trinidad Island for enemy vessels. If any were spotted, Captain Grant was to radio *H.M.S. Bristol* immediately.

Admiralty orders had specifically mentioned the possibility that *S.M.S. Dresden*, *S.M.S. Kronprinz Wilhelm*, and the *Cap Trafalgar* might be at or near the suspected rendezvous point. The *Carmania* was slower than any of those vessels, and Captain Grant and Commander Barr agreed that they needed some sort of advantage.

The solution was to effect a disguise. The only German vessel that the *Carmania* might resemble was the *Cap Trafalgar*. If the *Carmania* were to assume the identity of the German liner, she might be able to confuse any German warships she might encounter, giving her time either to come within firing range of an enemy ship or time to escape should she encounter a larger force.

Crewmen were put to work building a wooden frame and stretching deck awnings over it to create a third funnel for the *Carmania*. That night, only fifty miles from Trinidad Island, the officers celebrated Captain Grant's birthday. The ship's doctor proposed a toast to the ship herself, but wasn't sure whether to call her *H.M.S. Carmania* or the *Cap Trafalgar*. He settled instead on *H.M.S. Sybarite*, a commentary on the luxurious nature of a liner-turned-warship that served Scottish salmon and Dover sole and stocked Rothschild wine, fine cognac, and Havana cigars.

At Trinidad Island, *Cap Trafalgar* had undergone further changes, becoming more warlike. The armament from His Imperial Majesty's gunboat *Eber* had been transferred to *Cap Trafalgar*. The skipper of the *Eber*, *Korvettenkapitän* Julius Wirth, now assumed command of the liner and added his crew to the complement of the *Cap Trafalgar*.

The two newly installed 4.1-inch guns had a range of only 7,000 yards, and the six machine guns wouldn't be of much help except at close range. Langerhannsz therefore proposed a novel idea about how the *Cap Trafalgar* might engage the enemy if pressed into a fight. Demonstrating the ship's surprising agility, her former commanding officer suggested sprinting headlong toward the enemy and then swinging alongside to land boarding parties.

Lieutenant Commander Wirth continued to hold training exercises, perfecting the techniques that might save the undergunned *Cap Trafalgar* and even render her victorious in a one-on-one engagement. For his part, Captain Langerhannsz located an ancient field mortar on Trinidad Island and, after being politely denied permission to install it aboard the *Cap Trafalgar*, had the gun mounted in the bows of the collier *Eleonore Woermann*. His idea was to use the mortar to fire coal soaked in oil, setting fire to enemy vessels or, at the least, creating an impenetrable smokescreen.

Knowing that the British were probably at hand, Lieutenant Wirth had returned from patrol September 13 and was coaling his vessel. He meant to evacuate Trinidad Island as soon as possible. He had posted the *Eleonore Woermann* to the southwest of the island as a lookout. At 11:04 A.M., September 14, a strange ship hove into view on the northern horizon.

As the *Carmania* cleared Nine-Pin Peak, a large two-stacker painted in the familiar Cunard colors could be seen at anchor and taking on coal. Captain Barr tentatively identified the vessel as "one of ours."

On board the *Cap Trafalgar*, first officer Lieutenant Feddersen couldn't be sure of the newcomer's identity, and he suggested that she might be their sister ship, *Finisterre*. Not taking any chances, Wirth ordered his vessel to weigh anchor and signal for identification.

Captain Grant obliged, and as soon as his ensign had been run up, the *Cap Trafalgar* heeled about and charged toward the *Carmania*. As the latter drew near, Captain Grant fired a warning shot across her bow. The *Cap Trafalgar* returned fire, and the fight had begun.

The German gunners aimed at the *Carmania*'s bridge, quickly knocking out her communication system and killing one of the gun crews. Shots fired from the *Carmania* smacked into the *Cap Trafalgar*, starting fires and sending deadly splinters flying, one of which killed her helmsman.

His dummy bridge on fire, Lieutenant Commander Wirth worked to maintain his collision course, determined to come alongside and board the *Carmania*. In the confusion, however, the ship drifted, giving the British gunners the target they needed. Directed by Lieutenant Commander Lockyer, the *Carmania*'s first officer, round after round crashed into the *Cap Trafalgar*'s waterline.

The German liner began to list to starboard. In an effort to right his vessel, Wirth made a port turn—turning away from the *Carmania*. A well-placed shot from the *Cap Trafalgar* tore through the *Carmania*, and the resulting fire forced the evacuation of the ship's bridge.

With Captain Barr in charge of damage control parties, Captain Grant moved to a conning station aft. The destruction of the ship's communications systems necessitated a makeshift system, and commands were relayed to the engine room through a series of whistles.

Barr's work parties had almost succeeded in extinguishing the fires when Captain Grant changed course. Air rushed in from the opposite side of the *Carmania*, fanning the flames and further endangering the ship. Captain Barr rushed topside to see what was happening.

Steaming between the two burning liners, the coal ship *Eleonore Woermann* was approaching. Reminiscent of Admiral Farragut's standing in the rigging during the Battle of Mobile Bay, Captain Langerhannsz now positioned himself at the bow of the collier, hanging from a ladder next to his ancient mortar.

Cigar in hand, the German officer lit the mortar's fuse. A wall of flame erupted from the weapon, blanketing the area in a dense, greasy smokescreen, and Langerhannsz began reloading the old field piece.

On board the *Cap Trafalgar*, temporarily hidden from the guns of the *Carmania*, a mortally wounded Lieutenant Commander Wirth ordered his men to abandon ship. As soon as the men were overboard, Wirth dismissed his officers.

Aboard the *Carmania*, Commander Barr suggested there was no point in remaining on the scene. The *Cap Trafalgar* was doomed, and the *Eleonore Woermann* was busy picking up survivors. Accordingly, Captain Grant put about and had his men concentrate on extinguishing the fires. The eighty-minute battle was over.

The *Cap Trafalgar* momentarily righted herself and then began sinking by the bow. She remains the only passenger ship ever to be sunk by another passenger ship in battle.

The collier was able to rescue 286 crewmen. Casualties included twelve dead and three missing. Lieutenant Commander Wirth's body was recovered, and he was buried at sea the following day with military honors.

Limping away, the crippled *Carmania* had no bridge and no engine room controls. Casualties included nine dead and twenty-six wounded. The *Kronprinz Wilhelm* was sighted on the horizon, but the captain of that vessel, *Kapitänleutnant* Thierfelder, feared a possible nest of British warships and changed courses to avoid the *Carmania*.

The cruiser *H.M.S. Bristol* located the *Carmania* the following morning and helped extinguish the fires on board the liner. The cruiser *H.M.S. Cromwell* also arrived on scene, and between the two British warships, the *Carmania* was outfitted well enough to make it to Pernambuco, Brazil, for necessary repairs. Afterward, she steamed for Gibraltar and was back in service within two months.

Captain Langerhannsz was tried in Montevideo on the charge of misleading port authorities concerning armament aboard his former command. He was acquitted and interned in Argentina for the remainder of the war.

Captain Grant was dismissed from sea duties some time later due to poor health and retired as a rear admiral in 1920, just five weeks before his death from tuberculosis. Captain Barr commanded several more Cunard liners pressed into service as troopships. He retired in 1916.

The *Carmania* was honored in 1919 when the British Navy League presented the vessel with a silver plate from Lord Nelson's *H.M.S. Victory*. The liner was the only civilian ship to receive one of the plates.

The
Legend
Behind
Moby Dick

P ERHAPS ONE OF THE MOST haunting stories of the sea is Melville's classic *Moby Dick*, the tale of the malevolent milk-white whale and the obsessed Captain Ahab, sworn to kill the beast. In the dramatic conclusion of the novel Moby Dick smashes the whaler *Pequod* and tows Ahab to the depths of Davy Jones's locker, leaving a sole survivor, Ishmael, to recount the story.

Many of the details in the book that concern whaling and the whaleman's life came from Melville's own experience as an ordinary seaman, whaleman, and harpooner. After an initial flirtation with the merchant marine, Melville shipped out of Fairhaven aboard the whaler *Acushnet*.

The vessel rounded the Horn and cruised up the west coast of South America and then on to the Marquesas, where the young whaleman jumped ship to dally in paradise.

Next came duty aboard the whaler *Lucy Ann* bound for Tahiti, followed by a stint as harpooner aboard the *Charles and Henry*, until the ship put in at Honolulu. In these voyages, Melville became all too familiar with the grinding routine of shipboard life and the heart-stopping action of "darting the fish." But what was the inspiration for the book that has become to be regarded as his best work?

That a whale could sink a ship had been proven conclusively. In November 1819, a sperm whale had attacked the whaler *Essex* and sent her to the bottom in a matter of minutes. What followed was one of the most incredible open boat voyages every attempted, as the captain and his two mates steered their whaleboats for South America, some three thousand miles away.

While serving as a seaman aboard the *Acushnet*, Melville happened to meet the son of Owen Chase—the man who had been chief mate of the ill-fated *Essex*. Young Chase gave Melville a copy of his father's book describing his adventures, and Melville later wrote, "The reading of this wondrous story on the landless sea, and so close to the very latitude of the shipwreck, had a surprising effect on me."

Melville's other source of inspiration and the model for his mythic rogue whale were stories of Mocha Dick, a wily, hearty sperm whale that chewed up whaleboats as easily as if they were made of matchsticks.

Mocha Dick was so named because he was first reported near the island of Mocha, off the coast of Chile, in 1810. He was described as a big sperm whale, light gray in color (although some reports had him "white as wool," others "dazzling white" or "off white"). As the whaleboats drew near, the whalemen could make out an eight-foot scar across the monster's head. The giant whale had turned and attacked one of the whaleboats, smashing it to pieces. The legend had begun.

Some writers have suggested that it was Mocha Dick himself who sank the *Essex*, but this is probably wishful thinking. There is not any evidence to place the blame on Mocha Dick, other than that it was unusual for a whale to act in such a manner. Only Melville in his novel has successfully combined the story of the white whale and the sinking of a whaleship. We should leave it at that.

Mocha Dick was reported here and there over the years, smashing whaleboats, fouling harpoon lines, and killing the occasional whaleman who ventured too near. Yet it was not until the summer of 1840 that the leviathan went on a destructive rampage.

In July of that year, the English whaler *Desmond* was cruising the whaling grounds some two hundred miles off the coast of Chile. One of the mastheads gave the cry, "Thar she blows!" followed by, "Thar she breaches!" About two miles from the ship, an enormous sperm whale was flinging itself fully out of the water, then crashing mightily into the waves of the Pacific. Two boats were lowered and headed toward the lone whale.

Suddenly, the monster turned and began speeding toward the boats. As he approached, his large scar was plainly visible. The sailors pulled for their lives, but the whale was faster. He smashed into the lead boat, spilling its occupants overboard. The enraged beast chewed up the wreckage and then sounded, diving deep into the water.

Mocha Dick disappeared for fifteen minutes or so while the second whaleboat plucked the dazed survivors out of the sea. Then the whale smashed the remaining boat, coming straight up from the depths. Satisfied with his handiwork, Mocha Dick swam off placidly, leaving two dead men in his wake.

A month later and 500 miles to the south, the Russian whaler *Serepta* lowered two boats under similar circumstances—a lone whale sighted in the distance. One of the boat-steerers managed to land a harpoon, and the mate finished off the whale with his lance. By now, the boats were some three miles from the *Serepta*, and they began the long tow back to the ship. From nowhere surfaced the mighty Mocha Dick, breaching his seventy-foot length between the whaleboats and their mother ship. He took aim for the lead boat.

The vengeful whale easily destroyed the first boat and turned toward the second. The mate of the remaining whaleboat navigated it behind the dead whale for protection. Mocha Dick circled around until the whaleboat had to cut its line on the dead whale and dash back to the whaler. The Russians sailed off as Mocha Dick stood guard over his slain comrade.

In May 1841, as the *John Day*, out of Bristol, lay in the South Atlantic, Mocha Dick made a spectacular appearance some hundred yards away from the whaler. The concussion of the whale's body slamming into the water rocked the *John Day* as if she had been a toy boat in a child's bath.

Three boats were lowered, and, as he had done so often before, the dreaded whale charged the lead boat. The crew of the tiny whaleboat knew of Mocha Dick's habits, and they were ready for his onslaught. Dancing nimbly aside as the whale approached, the harpooner rammed home his dart and wound the line tightly around the boat's loggerhead.

The huge whale then took the whaleboat on a Nantucket sleigh ride, pulling the craft and crew at high speeds. The ride carried them three miles before Mocha Dick unexpectedly turned around and made for the attached whaleboat. Striking it broadside, the beast never slowed but swam over the boat and crushed it with an impudent slap of his flukes. Two men were missing.

The two surviving whaleboats closed on the killer, and, while the crew of one boat made fast the harpoon line, Mocha Dick stove in the bottom of the third boat. The second boat, at a signal from the captain, cut loose the line and picked up the survivors. Another battle had ended with Mocha Dick the victor.

In October 1842, Mocha Dick fought what whaling historians agree was his greatest battle. Sailing off the coast of Japan, a little lumber schooner became the object of the great whale's wrath. After breaching nearly two miles away from the harmless vessel, the whale sounded and reappeared in the ship's wake. To the horror of the crew, the leviathan sped headlong into the stern of the schooner, smashing it to pieces. The ship quickly took water and would have sunk had it not been for the cargo of lumber that kept her afloat. As water washed across her decks, three whalers appeared on the horizon.

The whaling captains held a quick conference and decided that the combined efforts of the three whalers, the Scottish ship *Crief*, the British *Dudley*, and the American vessel *Yankee*, could certainly put an end to one rogue whale's mischief. As the captains drew up their battle plans, Mocha Dick breached a mile to windward, seeming to stand on end before crashing down into the water.

Six whaleboats were lowered, two from each ship. The whale sounded and disappeared for twenty minutes while the whalemen waited tensely. Through the clear water, one of the crewmen spot-

Herman Melville, himself a former whaleman, combined the story of the sinking of the Essex *and the tales about Mocha Dick to create his masterpiece,* Moby Dick.

The rogue whale Mocha Dick waged a private war against whalers from 1810 until his death in 1859.

ted Mocha Dick swimming straight toward the boat. The oarsmen dug deep and pulled out of harm's way just as the terrible figure emerged from the depths. One of the *Yankee*'s whaleboats slid alongside the monster and planted a harpoon.

Mocha Dick seemed finally to have met his match. He let go a mighty spout and feebly wagged his flukes. He quivered a bit and then ceased moving altogether. The whalemen waited another five minutes to make sure the fabled beast was dead.

As they drew closer to the whale, Mocha Dick suddenly came to life, smashing one of the Scottish boats and slapping it with his flukes. He then made for one of the British boats, missed, and turned and caught it in his cruel jaws. He shook his mighty head, pulverizing the unfortunate boat and a couple of crewmen. Ignoring the other pesky whaleboats, Mocha Dick swam to the lumber schooner again and rammed into it a couple of times before sounding. Survivors were picked up from the wreckage.

As the wounded were being tended to aboard the *Crief*, Mocha Dick suddenly reappeared. He attacked the bow of the Scottish ship, shearing off its jib boom and bowsprit. Satisfied, he swam away windward, keeping a wary eye on the three whaleships. They offered no more resistance.

The rogue whale was heard from occasionally over the years. In all, he is credited with fighting some one hundred battles with whalers and commending at least thirty whalemen to the deep. His fame, of course, lives on through his fictional counterpart, Moby Dick.

Whatever happened to Mocha Dick? Several stories provide conflicting versions, but the most widely accepted claims that the old whale was harpooned and killed by the crew of a Swedish whaler in 1859, some nine years after Melville, in a burst of literary energy, wrote *Moby Dick*. According to the report, Mocha Dick hardly produced a struggle. He was blind in one eye and carried nineteen harpoon barbs in his blubber.

Across the
Pacific in
a Longboat

U SING AN OPEN FLAME to illuminate his path, the clipper's first mate made his way below deck to the varnish cask. He never had time to realize his mistake. Either the liquid or fumes from the cask ignited, sending a wall of flame roaring through the wooden ship.

The flames leapt up through an open hatch, gulping hungrily at the fresh night air and igniting rigging and masts. The crew responded quickly, but the fire was spreading too fast to be contained.

The order to abandon ship was given. Ten days' provisions, containers of water, and navigating instruments were collected hastily. In the confusion, the men smashed a hole in the side of the longboat as it and two smaller boats were lowered over the side. The sailors pulled mightily at the oars to escape the roaring inferno which a few minutes before had been a graceful sailing ship.

The *Hornet*, Josiah Mitchell commanding, had been beating her way north in the Pacific. She was on a four-month passage to San Francisco, having left New York some time before and safely rounding the Horn. Now she was gone, her crew and passengers deposited on the high seas. It was May 3, 1866.

As the sun crept over the eastern horizon, the men scanned their surroundings in vain, hoping that some other vessel had seen the fire during the night. When no rescuers appeared, Captain Mitchell rationed the food—two crackers and a pint of water daily—and set out for some deserted islands that lay to the north.

The ship had gone down in the doldrums, and not a breath of air stirred. Instead, the merciless sun beat down upon the crews of the three boats, which had been lashed together. The men valiantly took up the rowing, with Captain Mitchell at the tiller.

After a week at sea in the open boats, a full seven days of backbreaking labor at the oars, they had covered only three hundred miles. Someone in one of the smaller boats ate more than his allotted ration, causing hardship for his fellow sailors. Under the strain and the privation, mutinous talk broke out. The ship's boy alerted the captain, who, along with his two passengers, armed himself with a pistol. The crisis passed, but the two smaller boats were cast off.

The three vessels eventually became separated on the mountainous seas. Neither of the two smaller boats was ever seen again. The captain and his fellows in the twenty-one-foot longboat finally made the trade winds and set sail for the west. Now the fluky winds had been left behind, but so had the rain squalls, which had previously filled their water bottles.

Captain Mitchell steered for a group of islands that appeared on his charts as the American Group. The mythical isles supposedly lay halfway between the Revilla Gigedo Islands and the Hawaiian chain. One month and three days after abandoning the *Hornet*, the crew in the longboat reached the point where the American Group was supposed to be and found only wide-open ocean.

A lesser man might have given up at this point, but Captain Mitchell was made of stronger stuff. He swallowed his bitter disappointment and turned the boat's prow toward Hawaii. Running wildly before the wind, Mitchell and his charges were literally racing against time. Still more than twelve hundred miles from the Polynesian paradise, the hungry crew had run out of food and had only their belongings to eat—a few scraps of cloth, the leather of their shoes and belts, a little stale water, and the wood chips from the butter keg.

A week later, miraculously, the men still clung to life with grim determination. One of the two passengers, Henry Ferguson, was still enchanted with life enough to write, "Most lovely rainbow last evening, perfect bow very distinct. Certainly is a good sign. Saw new moon. God has spared us wonderfully to see it." The captain's journal reflects a similar optimism and trust in Providence:

> Six weeks in the boat today. Still running. Nothing to eat and water for one day more, yet I feel better than I could expect. Too weak to write. God has been very merciful. We may yet be preserved.

God saw fit to give them that "one day more," and on June 15, the longboat of the burned ship *Hornet* raised land. Some natives from the village of Laupahoehoe sighted the boat and, recognizing its plight, swam out to give assistance. They guided the longboat through the treacherous reefs surrounding the rugged cost, gently bringing it ashore.

All fifteen men in the boat had survived their grueling ordeal. The crew had established a record for the longest time afloat and the greatest distance covered by an open boat. They had traveled some four thousand miles in forty three days.

After resting at the village, the men were transported by their native hosts to Honolulu. There they told their amazing story to an eager young journalist visiting the islands.

Working as a correspondent for the Sacramento *Daily Union*, Mark Twain recognized the drama of the story of survival at sea and received an exclusive interview with the recuperating men. Later, Twain sold an article based on the diaries of the captain and the passengers to *Harper's* magazine, his first story to appear in a New York periodical. Twain later looked back at this as a turning point in his career, referring some thirty three years later to the event and its subsequent stories, as "My Debut as a Literary Person."

Though the men survived the voyage, all were deeply affected by their harrowing experience. Captain Mitchell returned to sea, but apparently never fully regained his strength. One of the two passengers, Samuel Ferguson, died shortly after reaching California (he

Mark Twain turned a true tale of survival at sea into his "debut as a literary person."

already suffered from tuberculosis). The other passenger, Samuel's brother Henry, returned to the East Coast and eventually became and Episcopalian priest.

As for the longboat, which had so faithfully served the survivors of the *Hornet*, she was sold to a Frenchman in Hilo for $200.

The Gentlemanly War of Commander Karl von Müller

ARLY ON THE MORNING OF August 14, 1914, Fregattenkap-
itän Karl von Müller directed his warship, *S.M.S. Emden*, and her collier *Markomannia*, south-southwest,
veering away from the rest of German Vice Admiral von
Spee's East Asiatic Squadron, which was headed due east from Pagan
Island toward distant South America. Just two days before, von
Müller had received permission to wage his own war in the Indian
Ocean, an area dominated by the British. It would have been too
dangerous for the entire German squadron to steam into those
waters, but one ship alone might have a fighting chance.

The *Emden*, a *Dresden*-class light cruiser, had been laid down by
Kaiserliche Werft in Danzig in 1906 and was launched two years
later. She was the last piston-engined cruiser ever built in Germany
and cost a total of 6.4 million gold marks. The *Emden* measured 395
feet in length with a beam of forty-four feet. Her armament consisted of ten rapid-fire, 4.13-inch guns; eight five-pounders and two
torpedo tubes. With a top speed of twenty-five knots, the agile ship
would be able to chase down merchantmen and, it was hoped,
outrace pursuers.

The first few days of the cruise were fairly uneventful. The

Emden called at the bombarded German radio station at Yap, northeast of the Palau Islands, and over the next few days met up with other German vessels, directing them to safe harbors.

Eight days out, the cruiser crossed the equator and, by radio, set up a rendezvous with the German steamer *Tannenfels*, arranging to take on fresh supplies and coal. Upon arrival at their meeting point at Timor, the *Tannenfels* was not to be found. Several hours later, the Dutch battleship *Tromp* appeared, warning off the *Emden*. The same vessel had discovered the *Tannenfels* earlier and had enforced the Netherlands' rule of neutrality by escorting her to international waters.

Commander von Müller steamed in an easterly direction until the *Tromp* was out of sight, then reversed his course and headed in the direction of Bali.

It was at this point that *Kapitänleutnant* Hellmuth von Mücke, the *Emden*'s first officer, devised a clever disguise for the warship, much like the one that would be effected soon by the British cruiser *Carmania*, half a world away. The *Emden*'s profile prominently featured three smokestacks, the signature of a German light cruiser. Von Mücke suggested that the crew build a false funnel of wood and canvas, making the vessel look like a British cruiser. The captain agreed, and the fourth stack, an oval in design, was added in line with the three round stacks.

On September 3, the German ship passed within shelling distance of *H.M.S. Hampshire*, but the British cruiser paid no attention to her German counterpart, and von Müller continued his coaling. Six days later, the raider came across her first prize, the Greek steamer *Pontoporos*. The merchantman, which carried a cargo of 6,500 tons of coal from Calcutta, was boarded by a prize crew and pressed into German service.

Basing their next actions on sailing schedules found on board the Greek cargo ship, the *Emden*, *Markomannia*, and *Pontoporos* moved into position to intercept vessels on the Colombo-Calcutta route. They were rewarded on the morning of September 10 by the appearance of the British passenger freighter, *S.S. Indus*.

The freighter captain, Smaridge, made the fatal mistake of

The soft-spoken Commander Karl von Müller was honored for his gallantry and daring by both sides during and after World War I.

SMS Emden *was the last piston-engined cruiser built in Germany.*

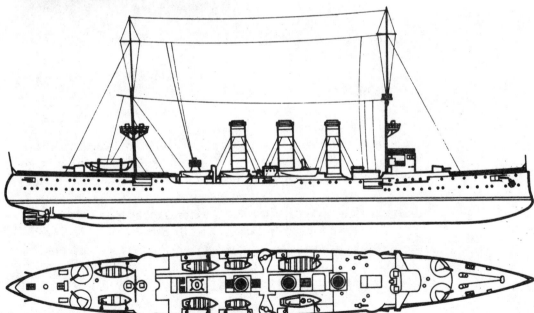

thinking the *Emden* was a British cruiser and allowed the warship to come in too close. Prize officer Julius Lauterbach took temporary command of the *Indus*, and the British crew was transferred to the coal ship *Markomannia*. The Germans took what they wanted from the *Indus*, and the ship was sunk. The *Emden* was in business.

Next morning brought the British ship *Lovat* to the *Emden*. The *Lovat* was on her way to Bombay to pick up troops for the war effort. Her officers and crew were placed aboard the *Markomannia*, and the *Lovat* followed the *Indus* to the bottom of the sea.

The third day of serious hunting produced a third British freighter, this one the 4,657-ton *Kabinga*, bound for New York carrying a cargo of jute. The *Emden* captured her and placed the British crews from the *Indus* and *Lovat* aboard, along with a German prize crew.

At 2:00 A.M. on the thirteenth, the German raider successfully captured the Scottish collier *Killin* and sank her at 10:00 A.M. That afternoon, the *Emden* intercepted, captured, and sank the 7,600-ton steamer *Diplomat*. The neutral Italian ship *Loredano* was intercepted but allowed to go her way. Unfortunately for the crew of the *Emden*, the *Loredano* passed on the news of the German raider's presence. The Royal Navy responded by temporarily halting shipping along the Colombo-Singapore routes.

The next day von Müller captured the 4,000 ton collier *Trabboch* and sank her. The *Kabinga* was now crowded with the crews of the captured or sunk vessels. Commander von Müller set the *Kabinga* at liberty not far from the mouth of the river Hooghly, and, to his surprise, his former prisoners accorded the German officer three cheers as the *Emden* steamed away.

Shortly after freeing his captives, von Müller intercepted another Scottish vessel, the *Clan Matheson*, bound for Calcutta with a cargo of Rolls-Royces, locomotive engines, and a thoroughbred racehorse. In less than an hour, the merchantman lay at the bottom of the ocean. The next day, her crew was transferred to the Norwegian freighter *Dovre* for safe passage. The British captain, W. Harris, shook hands with von Müller and thanked him for the courteous and humane way in which he and his crew had been treated.

Word of von Müller's daring and his chivalric ways spread

around the world. Despite their heavy merchant marine losses to the *Emden*, the British admired the dashing von Müller. As one British pursuer admitted, "We admire her [*Emden*'s] exploits as much as we wish the ship may be taken." In the Fatherland, the forty-one-year-old von Müller was held up as an example of German superiority, and an adoring public waited anxiously for further tales of his adventures.

The Allied fleets in the Indian Ocean were busy, too. During the cruise of the *Emden*, no fewer than eighty warships were engaged in the hunt for the raider. No doubt to his amusement, von Müller intercepted numerous radio communiqués between the vessels searching for the cruiser, including one incredible transmission from a shore station that asked, "*Emden*, where are you?"

In fact, the *Emden* was hunting for new prey south of Calcutta. The *Pontoporos* was dispatched to Simalur Island while *Emden* proceeded toward Rangoon, searching in vain for more merchantmen. Then von Müller suddenly changed tactics. Where was it written that all his raids had to be carried out against other vessels?

The captain quickly formulated a plan for attacking the port installations at Madras. The raider steamed west across the Bay of Bengal toward her destination. At 9:45 P.M. on September 22, the *Emden* lay two miles off the coast. The first of her shells screamed across the night sky to rain destruction upon the unsuspecting city. The primary targets of the evening were the large tanks of the Burmah Oil Company. After dumping 125 projectiles on the city in a ten-minute period, the *Emden* slipped away in the night.

Von Müller took his vessel around Ceylon and, on the twenty-fifth, intercepted the British steamer *King Lud*. She carried no cargo but was relieved of her provisions and sent to the bottom. At ten that night, the 3,014–ton *Tymeric*, carrying 4,600 tons of sugar for England, was boarded by a prize crew. The ship's captain, J. J. Tulloch, refused to cooperate with the raiders and ordered his men to resist the Germans.

Von Müller had the captain and first officer arrested and placed aboard the *Emden* and the crew transferred to the *Markomannia* without the benefit of keeping any of their personal possessions. The ship was sunk immediately, in view of the searchlights of the port of Colombo.

A few hours later, early on the morning of the twenty-sixth, the *Emden* stopped yet another ship, the *Gryfevale*, which was to be made a liberty ship for the crews of the *King Lud* and the *Tymeric*. At about 2:30 A.M. of the twenty-seventh, the *Emden* took a well-met prize, the collier *Buresk*, fully loaded with 6,600 tons of Welsh coal. Von Müller gladly added the vessel to his flotilla. The next day, the German raider captured and sank another steamer, the 3,500-ton *Ribera*. Just after dark, another prize appeared, the British freighter *Foyle*. She was duly captured and sunk. The *Gryfevale* was now released, and the former captives offered three cheers for von Müller, three cheers for the German officers, and three cheers for the crew of the *Emden*.

The *Emden* now headed for the Maldives for a little rest and refitting. The ship took her last load of coal from the *Markomannia*, and the collier was dispatched to a rendezvous point with the *Pontoporos*. The latter was to be paid off and allowed to resume her voyage.

Von Müller made for the lonely outpost of Diego Garcia. The inhabitants there had no knowledge of the war, and the Germans did not enlighten them, instead taking advantage of their hospitality, scraping and repainting the *Emden* and taking on board a good supply of fresh fruit and vegetables, fish, and a live pig.

The *Emden*'s phenomenal success continued, as the raider captured more ships: the *Clan Grant*, the *Ponrabbel*, the *Benmohr*, the *Troilus*, the *St. Egbert*, and the *Exford*. On the morning of October nineteenth, the German warship encountered the 5,114–ton *Chilkana*, the thirteenth victim of the *Emden* since the bombardment of Madras. The *St. Egbert* was released as a liberty ship with some 600 former prisoners aboard.

While the decks of the *Emden* often resembled a barnyard, with livestock milling about and confiscated cargo stacked high, the men themselves enjoyed such luxuries as coffee, cigars, candy, and liquor that had been "liberated" from the Allied ships. One officer later recalled, "Sometimes I felt as if I were at a great fair. Hams dangled from the engine skylight. There were stacks of chocolate and bottles labeled 'Cognac' with three stars."

Von Müller again changed tactics by steaming out of the way of potential prizes and letting ships pass in the night unchallenged. The daring officer had a new plan—a bold raid on the island of Penang, near the northwest coast of Malaya.

Upon nearing the island, which served as a port of call for Allied warships, von Müller once more put up the false fourth smokestack and ran up the British ensign. The cruiser blithely passed a pilot boat in the harbor and then struck the Union Jack, replacing it with the German battle colors. In a matter of minutes, the *Emden* had fired two fatal torpedoes and a torrent of shells into the anchored Russian cruiser *Zhemtchug* and sent her to the bottom. The raider sped out of port before most observers knew what was happening.

The French torpedo boat destroyer *Mousquet* approached the *Emden* even as the latter had stopped a British steamer to apologize for firing upon an unarmed harbor boat by mistake and to explain why the raider had not stayed behind to help rescue survivors from the Russian warship. The *Emden* fired upon the French ship from 4,500 yards, and soon the destroyer was sinking.

One officer and thirty–five crewmen were rescued, but two of the badly wounded died during the night. Von Müller buried the sailors at sea with full military honors. On the thirtieth, the *Emden* intercepted the British steamer *Newburn* and asked that she take the French prisoners to Sumatra for medical treatment.

After a coaling rendezvous with the *Buresk* on the last day of October, von Müller turned the raider toward the Cocos (Keeling) Islands. His objective there was the British telegraph and radio station on Direction Island.

Early on the morning of November 9, the *Emden* reached the island. A landing party of fifty was dispatched to destroy the station. Unbeknownst to the Germans, their approach had been seen, and the radio station had relayed the urgent message, "*Emden* here, *Emden* here," for fifteen minutes, until the sailors landed.

The landing party, under the direction of first officer von Mücke, set foot on the island and met no resistance. The manager of the station, Mr. D. A. G. de H. Farrant, approached the Germans and offered his hand and his congratulations. When questioned why, the manager replied that Commander von Müller had been awarded the Iron Cross, First and Second Class, and the other officers had been awarded the Iron Cross, Second Class, with fifty Second Class crosses to be awarded at the captain's discretion.

The detachment went about its work destroying the station in an orderly manner. A "hurry up" message was relayed from the *Emden*, and as the landing party climbed back into its two cutters, the cruiser weighed anchor and began steaming away.

The reason for the raider's premature departure was the approach of the Australian cruiser *Sydney*, which sported six-inch guns. The *Emden*'s top speed was slower than that of the *Sydney*, and her four-inch guns had a shorter range than those of the Australian ship, leaving von Müller with precious few choices.

The Germans fired four salvos at the *Sydney*, scoring with the last. The Australian warship retreated beyond the *Emden*'s range and began pelting her with round after round. Von Müller kept trying to dance his ship out of harm's way, but death rained from the sky, and in less than two hours, the *Emden* had been run aground on North Keeling Island. The *Sydney* departed to chase down the collier *Buresk*.

While the battle between the *Emden* and *Sydney* still raged over the horizon, first officer *Lieutenant* Hellmuth von Mücke quickly reviewed his options. It was obvious from the sound of the guns that the *Emden*'s opponent was a heavier ship and that the German warship would likely be the loser in a one-on-one duel. Lieutenant von Mücke considered putting up a fight whenever the victorious Allied ship arrived, but such action seemed pointless.

One other option remained. A small, three-masted schooner, the *Ayesha*, lay in port. It had been von Mücke's original intention to destroy the vessel, but now he took a steam launch out to inspect the schooner, ostensibly searching for weapons. The captain and sole sailor aboard were taken off while von Mücke conducted his survey.

The British on the island had described the schooner as unseaworthy, but she looked sound to the German, so he immediately commandeered her for service in the Imperial German Navy.

The detachment from the *Emden* began gathering a stock of supplies from the island and transferring them to the *Ayesha*. Von Mücke apologetically took half of the islander's food stocks and foraged such personal items as tobacco, pipes, and other goods.

By the end of the day, the *Ayesha* was outfitted for sailing. With the German war flag flying and under tow by the steam launch, the schooner made her way out to sea. In the tradition of the best raider captains, von Mücke had voiced one plan of action within earshot of his enemies and now undertook quite another. He had led those on the island to believe that his detachment would sail for German East Africa, but actually he headed for the Dutch East Indies.

The *Sydney* had now steamed to Direction Island to capture the landing party, but to the Australians' surprise, there were no Germans on the island. The cruiser returned to the scene of the wrecked *Emden*. As the German battle flag still flew defiantly, *Sydney* fired again upon the disabled cruiser. Von Müller ran up a white flag at once. His casualties included 141 dead and sixty–five wounded.

The cruise of the *Emden* was over. She had traveled 30,000 miles, sunk or captured twenty three merchant vessels, sunk two warships, and destroyed some £15 million, almost $73 million, worth of cargo, while inflicting a minimum of casualties and sustaining only one until the day of her final battle.

The destination of the overcrowded *Ayesha* was Padang. Von Mücke still maintained hope that somehow the *Emden* had escaped destruction and would head for a similar safe harbor. In the meanwhile, the crew of fifty was organized in two watches, each under the supervision of an ensign, and the vessel was put in order. While most of the enlisted men themselves were ignorant in the ways of sailing, the officers had served aboard training sailers and could direct the men in their duties.

The *Ayesha* made between three and eight knots and was frequently becalmed during her passage. Two weeks had passed quietly when, on November 23, 1914, land was sighted. *Lieutenant* von Mücke and a small party went ashore to establish their position.

Their navigation had been right on target; they had reached the island of Siberut, almost due west of Padang. Two days later, the crew was rewarded with its first view of the island of Sumatra.

On the morning of the twenty-seventh, the Dutch destroyer *Lynx* approached the *Ayesha*. Aboard the schooner, honors were piped and the German flag dipped in salute. The *Lynx* returned the honor, and von Mücke went aboard the Dutch ship in full uniform, complete with sword.

While discussing his plan to call at the harbor of Emmahaven, *Lieutenant* von Mücke learned the fate of the *Emden* from the captain of the *Lynx*. Von Mücke sent a message to the Dutch neutrality officer to the effect that the *Ayesha* was in port for emergency reasons and needed to take on fresh supplies. German merchantmen in port sent gifts of food, beer, and extra clothing to the men aboard the schooner.

An argument as to the nature of the vessel arose, the Dutch claiming that the *Ayesha* was a prize and could be forced to stay in port. Von Mücke argued that the schooner was a German warship and was entitled to a twenty-four-hour stay in neutral waters. Von Mücke finally prevailed, and once he was successful in secretly passing a message to the port's German consul requesting that a German steamer meet the *Ayesha* at a predetermined point, the officer gave the order to sail.

Just outside territorial waters, the men on the schooner were hailed from a rowboat. Two men of the German Naval Reserve had followed from Padang and begged permission to join the *Emden* detachment. Leutnant Willmann and Machinist's Mate First Class Schwaneberger swelled the number of the crew to fifty–two as the *Ayesha* set a southerly course.

On December 9, a British steamer apparently sighted the *Ayesha* and duly reported the sighting to British authorities. Five days later the schooner rendezvoused with the German collier *Choising*, the steamer dispatched by the German consul at Padang. Rough weather prevented a close approach, but on December 16, the officers and men of *S.M.S. Ayesha* went aboard the *Choising*. After sailing 1,710 nautical miles in the service of the Kaiser's Navy, the little schooner was sent to the bottom as her former crewmen accorded her three cheers.

Like the memorable *Judea*, the ill-fated collier in Joseph Conrad's "Youth," the *Choising* had been plagued with spontaneous combustion problems during her eastern voyage, and she was blackened from smoke and fire. The crippled vessel could barely make eight knots, and it was decided that the safest course of action was to make for the closest German-allied soil, Turkish-ruled Arabia.

Disguised as the Italian steamer *Shenir*, the *Choising* avoided regular commerce lanes, choosing instead to wallow along below the Equator toward East Africa. *Kapitän* F. Minkwitz, master of the *Choising*, guided his limping vessel into the Gulf of Aden and then the Red Sea, landing the detachment and two of the *Choising*'s officers, Reserve *Leutnant* Geerdts and ship's doctor Henreich Lang, near Al Hudaydah, Yemen, on January 9, 1915.

The Germans soon found themselves surrounded by a ragtag band of Bedouins, and eventually a column of Turkish soldiers appeared to escort the sailors into town. The officers were welcomed by the Turkish authorities, who assured them that further travel by water was unadvisable since the British and French were maintaining a blockade some fifty miles up the coast.

When he inquired about overland travel, von Mücke received conflicting answers. The local administrator and the garrison commander insisted overland travel to Al Ula was quite possible. There, they said, Lieutenant von Mücke and his men would be able to continue their journey by rail. Subordinate Turkish officers, however, argued strongly against any such action.

In accordance with prearranged plans, von Mücke signaled to Captain Minkwitz that the services of the *Choising* were no longer required, and the vessel steamed for Massawa to sit out the war.

Without a ship, von Mücke was now committed to continuing his journey overland. The detachment stayed in the port city for two and a half weeks, during which time the Turks tried various methods of inducing the Germans not to leave. Apparently, the Turks believed that the sailors would be of help in putting down an insurrection by the locals, should one occur.

Finally, on January 27, the detachment and their Turkish guides set off for Sanaa, a hundred miles away across jagged mountains and unforgiving desert. The men rode donkeys while their equipment was transported by camels.

Because of the intense heat during the day, the column traveled by night. On their second night out, the Germans were approached by would-be robbers. One look at the menacing Maxim machine guns, however, was enough to drive away the bandits.

The sailors reached Sanaa on February 6. After many long and frustrating arguments with the local authorities and a flood of telegrams, it was decided that there was no way out of the city other than the way they had come, so the weary detachment headed once more for the oppressive environment of Al Hudaydah.

Von Mücke secretly hired a couple of small dhows and, on March 14, set sail up the Red Sea, escaping the conniving Turks who sought to keep the Germans in Yemen.

Three days later catastrophe nearly struck when one of the dhows hit a submerged reef and sank. All the men were rescued and transferred to the remaining dhow, the smaller of the two. Much of the stores had to be jettisoned to keep the overladen boat afloat. Two Maxim machine guns were recovered from the wreck, and the sailors reached Al Qunfidah on March 18.

A larger dhow was hired, and the detachment set sail again the next day, arriving at Al Lith five days later. Now they had no choice but to continue overland to the railhead at Al Ula. On March 27, Seaman Kiel died of typhus, the first casualty of the original *Emden* landing party. The sailor was buried at sea with military honors. The following evening, equipped with ninety camels, the Germans continued their journey toward Jiddah.

Riding from the afternoon hours until mid-morning, the detachment made good progress, coming to within a day's ride of Jiddah after three days of travel. Suddenly, at daybreak, the Germans were attacked by a group of Bedouins. As the sun rose, the sailors discovered they were surrounded by some 300 Arabs. The four Maxims were hurriedly set up. Other arms included thirteen rifles taken from the *Emden*, thirteen rifles supplied by the Turks, and some two dozen pistols.

Von Mücke led several bayonet charges against their attackers, killing fifteen bandits and sustaining one wounded sailor. He then attempted to retreat toward the sea but once more came under heavy fire. One sailor was killed and an officer badly wounded. Again, the deadly Maxims were put into use, silencing the guns of the Arabs.

A message was relayed to von Mücke that he and his men could have safe passage if they paid a ransom of £11,000, the equivalent of $53,532, and turned over all arms, camels, food, and water. The proud officer sent back a contemptuous answer and told his men to fortify their positions as best they could.

The wounded officer, *Leutnant* Schmidt, died that evening. Dawn brought a fresh attack from the tops of the dunes, and the machine guns held off the superior forces of the Bedouins. That night, the wounded sailor, Lanig, succumbed to his wounds. Lieutenant von Mücke sent two of his Arab guides, disguised as Bedouins, to Jiddah for help.

About mid-morning on April 3, the sound of gunfire in the distance heartened the Germans. A messenger from the Bedouins now told von Mücke and his men that they could keep their supplies and arms if only they would pay a ransom of £22,000, twice as much as demanded originally. The officer later wrote, "My answer is not worthy of mention."

And then, as suddenly as they had come, their attackers disappeared. An hour later, two men identifying themselves as messengers from the Emir of Mecca approached and promised safe passage with the Emir's son, Abdullah, to Jiddah. Although von Mücke was able to establish that the "rescue" had been a sham, he could not discover the reason for it, and the sailors were escorted courteously and safely into Jiddah.

Even as they feasted richly in the city, von Mücke made arrangements to continue the journey. Nothing could tempt him to continue his voyage overland, not even the presence of British ships of war. The officer hired a large dhow and set sail from Jiddah on April

8. They passed unnoticed through the blockade line, finally reaching Al Wajh, a hundred miles from the railhead at Al Ula.

The local authority, Suleiman Pasha, proved to be a man of honor and agreed to escort the sailors to the railhead. On May 7, 1915, Lieutenant von Mücke and the long-suffering detachment from the *Emden* rode into Al Ula.

From there, the men traveled by train through Arabia, Jordan, Syria, and Turkey to Constantinople where they received a hero's welcome. After many stops along the way, and many feasts, speeches, and celebrations, the detachment reached the Haydar Pasha station on May 23, 1915. Wearing new uniforms and the Iron Crosses they had all been awarded, the forty-nine officers and men stepped off the train to meed Admiral Wilhelm Souchon and the staff officers who awaited them.

The ensign from the *Emden* flew proudly from a boathook pole as *Kapitänleutnant* Hellmuth von Mücke saluted the admiral and said, "Beg to report, landing party from *S.M.S. Emden* numbering five officers, seven petty officers, and thirty-seven men, present and correct."

As for the captured commanding officer of the *Emden*, Commander von Müller was imprisoned during the war at Malta, then England, and finally in the Netherlands. He was recognized around the world as a gentleman in a time gone mad, and he was hailed as a hero by both sides. Germany bestowed the Order Pour le Merite—the Blue Max—upon the officer, who was promoted to full captain and given an administrative position in the Navy Office after the war.

The
Forgotten
Admiral
Blake

A SKED TO NAME THE greatest figures from Britain's storied list of seafarers, armchair students of naval history would suggest Lord Nelson, Sir Francis Drake, Captain Cook, Lord St. Vincent, perhaps, and possibly Lord Cochrane. Chances are the name of Admiral Robert Blake would not come up, yet he was one of the world's most influential naval officers and tacticians.

It was Admiral Blake who introduced the famous *Articles of War*, the basis of naval discipline, and his *Fighting Instructions* dominated naval tactics for more than a hundred years. The reason Blake's name is not familiar is that he was a Briton who dared to take up arms against the monarchy. Blake served under Oliver Cromwell during the English Civil War.

Robert Blake was born in Bridgwater, England, in 1598, the son of a wealthy merchant. He attended St. Alban's and Wadham Colleges at Oxford, then apparently returned home and took over the family business. Nothing else was recorded of his life until the outbreak of the Civil War.

Blake fought against the Royalists and proved himself an able general, defending Bristol against Prince Rupert in 1643, and defending Lyme the following year. In 1644, Blake occupied Taunton and held the town for two years. In 1645, he was reelected to Parliament, and in 1648, Blake organized the Commonwealth forces in Somerset.

It was not until February 1649 that Blake assumed his duties at sea, at the age of fifty. He was appointed "commissioner to command the fleet."

Two months later, Blake's first engagement at sea pitted him against Rupert's squadron. The plucky admiral blockaded the prince's forces for six months. Prince Rupert escaped, only to be hounded by Blake all the way to Portugal. The King of Portugal granted the English prince safe harbor, and the enraged admiral responded by capturing six ships and three Portuguese vessels returning from Brazil.

Blake continued prowling for Rupert in the Mediterranean. He succeeded in destroying the Royalist squadron in November 1650, and in the following spring, the admiral captured Britain's Scilly Isles, which had been in the hands of Royalist privateers.

The last strongholds of the Royalists had been destroyed. Shortly afterward, Blake was made a member of the Council of State.

In the meantime, tensions between England and the Netherlands were building. In 1651, the Council of State passed a Navigation Act that allowed only English-built-and-owned vessels to trade in English ports. The English fleet was also given the authority to engage foreign ships that refused to strike their ensigns upon encountering British men-of-war.

The Dutch began building additional warships to patrol the Channel, and in the spring of 1652, matters came to a head. Captain Anthony Young, aboard the Commonwealth Navy ship *President*, along with two other small English vessels, approached a number of Dutch ships and demanded the "proper" salute. One of the Dutchmen complied, but the others refused. After more demands and refusals, Young loosed a broadside toward the foreign vessels, and the fire was returned. One man aboard the *President* was killed, more verbal fencing ensued, and everyone sailed away fairly satisfied.

Farther up the Channel, the English fleet under Blake and the

Dutch fleet under Lieutenant Admiral Maarten Harpertszoon Tromp were anchored within sight of one another. Nine ships under English Rear Admiral Nehemiah Bourne were in the Downs, off the coast of Kent. The other twelve English ships were anchored to the west, in Rye Bay. The Dutch fleet, some forty-two vessels in all, was anchored between the two arms of the English fleet, off Dover. Despite Admiral Tromp's assurance that his fleet was anchored there only for shelter, the English were nervous.

The castle at Dover fired a few experimental shots in Tromp's direction; the English wanted the Dutchman to salute the English flag flying above the castle. Interested by the cannon fire, the two halves of the English fleet began converging on the Dutch fleet. Showing good sense, Tromp had his vessels weigh anchor and turn toward France. Something would change his mind, however.

A young Dutch captain named Joris Van der Saanen boarded Tromp's fifty-four-gun *Brederode* and informed the admiral of that morning's action by the *President*. Reportedly, Van der Saanen also told Tromp that the English fleet intended to capture the Dutch merchant fleet. There was no evidence to support the young captain's claim, but Tromp took his officer at his word.

The admiral ordered his fleet to come about and bear down on the approaching English fleet. His flagship flew a blood-red ensign, the signal for battle.

The English fired the first broadside; the battle had begun. Bourne managed to bring in his ships from the Downs for a flank attack on the Dutch fleet while Blake, aboard the forty-eight-gun *James*, continued to batter away at the head of the fleet. At nightfall, the Dutch fleet crept away toward home, leaving behind two vessels unable to sail, the *St. Maria* and the *St. Laurens*, the latter of which was towed back to England as a war prize.

Cromwell then began his war preparations: impressing able-bodied men between the ages of fifteen and fifty, speeding up ship-building, readying supplies, and conferring with Blake. The admiral reorganized the Navy into three squadrons—Red, White, and Blue. Blake sailed with the Red Squadron to the north to attack the Dutch herring fleet and to intercept homeward-bound Dutch Indiamen attempting to avoid the English Channel.

Blake made short work of the herring fleet and their twelve escorting warships, capturing most of the boats and relieving them of their catches. He released them with a warning to stay out of Scottish and English waters.

Tromp had sailed to engage Blake in the fishing grounds, but the two fleets had passed each other in the night. Then in a raging North Sea storm, the Dutch fleet suffered losses of greater than fifty percent, losing fifty-eight of ninety-two ships. Tromp was temporarily replaced by a surly Dutch officer, Admiral Witte de With.

Tromp eventually returned to head the Dutch Navy, but Blake beat him at almost every turn. Only once did it look as though Tromp had the upper hand—he met Blake's fleet of forty-two men-of-war with an impressive showing of 107 warships. Out of the apparent crushing defeat at the hands of the Dutch, Blake emerged with some new ideas about naval discipline. These he set down in the *Articles of War*, which established for the first time a definite code of conduct for officers and men.

Two months later, the two admirals crossed swords again under more equal odds—seventy-five Dutch ships to Blake's seventy. The new discipline in the English Navy was apparent, and heavy damage was inflicted upon the Dutch. Blake himself was severely wounded by a piece of flying iron, but he refused to go below decks, insisting instead upon leading the battle. The English had behaved and fought well, but Blake was increasingly aware of the free-for-all nature of naval battles.

The result of Blake's thoughts on the matter was a series of fourteen *Fighting Instructions* that outlined specific tactics and maneuvers, including the first mention of forming a line of battle at sea—the naval fighting formation that would be used until the time of Lord Nelson. Because of Blake, each captain would know precisely what to do in almost any given situation.

After the publication of the *Fighting Instructions*, the English rapidly dispatched the Dutch. The well-disciplined and organized English Navy was clearly superior to any other force then at sea. The

Admiral Robert Blake brought discipline to the English Navy but today is largely forgotten.

Before Blake's Fighting Instructions, *naval battles were little more than floating free-for-alls.*

last great battle between the two navies took place on August 10, 1653. The battle lines stretched out for sixteen miles for some 240 ships that did battle that day. Admiral Tromp was killed in the heavy action. The Dutch lost thirteen ships and suffered casualties in excess of 4,000. The English lost only two ships and about 1,000 men.

The English were now masters of the sea, and they completely ruled the Channel. Blake set up a blockade of the Netherlands, and according to one contemporary writer, that country was reduced to a land full of beggars.

A treaty was signed at Westminster in April 1654. The Dutch were surprised at Cromwell's generosity. English trade was still restricted, and foreign vessels still had to recognize the English ensign, but Cromwell saw no reason to punish the Dutch. He wanted the two countries to dwell together in peace.

The only real change brought about by the English Civil War was how naval warfare was to be fought. It was Blake who introduced fair and uniform discipline into the English Navy, and it was Blake who devised the brilliantly simple fighting tactics that would serve his navy so well for the next 100 years.

Admiral Blake continued his service in the Navy, fighting incredible campaigns against Tunisian corsairs, destroying land fortresses from the sea, and capturing enormous treasures. At Tenerife, Blake destroyed the entire Spanish fleet, losing only one ship and fifty men.

On August 7, 1657, just an hour before his victorious fleet sailed into Plymouth, the great Admiral Blake died of complications caused by his old wound. His body lay in state at Greenwich before receiving a state burial at Westminster Abbey. He was hailed as the greatest naval officer England had ever known.

In 1661, Charles II regained the throne from which his predecessor had been so undecorously removed, and it went out of vogue to praise those who had served under Cromwell. Admiral Blake's body was exhumed from Westminster Abbey and unceremoniously dumped into a pit, along with the bodies of other prominent Cromwellians. It was an ignoble fate for such a great officer. Admiral Blake was almost lost to obscurity, despite his accomplishments and lasting contributions to the service.

Forty Fathoms Down

THE MORNING OF May 23, 1939, looked promising to Lieutenant Oliver F. Naquin, commanding officer of the U.S. submarine *Squalus* (SS-192). The boat was to make her nineteenth and final test dive, the "Secretary of the Navy Dive," so-called because the submarine would be undergoing the tests dictated by the secretary, submerging to periscope depth, about sixty feet, in sixty seconds, while maintaining a forward speed of sixteen knots. "Nake," as his friends called the red-haired officer, felt confident since the crew had come within two seconds of that goal on the previous dive.

Commissioned March 1, 1939, *Squalus* was the newest and largest submarine in the fleet. She weighed 1,450 tons, measured 310 feet in length, and had a beam of twenty-seven feet. On the surface, she could race at speeds of twenty knots and could maintain speeds of nearly nine knots when submerged. She had cost some $4.5 million to build, and she represented the best of the Navy.

On that Tuesday morning, *Squalus* carried a complement of fifty-nine, including five officers, a crew of fifty-one, and three civilian observers. She had cast off from Portsmouth (New Hampshire) Navy Yard at 7:30 A.M., glided down the Piscataqua River, and

ABOVE: The submarine rescue ship USS Falcon, *left, and the submarine* USS Sculpin Squalus!'*s survivors.* OFFICIAL U.S. NAVY PHOTOGRAPH. *RIGHT: Lieutenant Oliver F. Naquin,* PHOTO COURTESY U.S. NAVAL ACADEMY.

past the Isles of Shoals. At 8:00 A.M., the quartermaster noted in his log, "Whaleback Light abeam to port, distance 1 mile." Ten minutes later, the boat's captain issued the order, "Rig for diving! Rig for diving!"

As soon as the order was given, the men raced to their work. Levers, indicators, valves, the Kingstons, RPM counters, gauges for depth and pressure, voltage meters, all were checked in rapid succession. By 8:25, Lieutenant William T. Doyle, the diving officer and second in command, was satisfied that the submarine was rigged for diving and relayed the message to Lieutenant Naquin who was on the bridge atop the conning tower. The bow planes swung out from the hull, and Nake ordered a message to be radioed to Portsmouth that *Squalus* was beginning her dive and would be under about an hour.

The skipper gave the order to dive, waited until he felt the massive diesels shut down and the ballast tanks flooding, and then

ticipated in the historic rescue of the
·manding officer of USS Squalus.

dropped through the hatch, dogging it tight behind him. The sound
of the diving horn blasted through the boat as Lieutenant Doyle
guided the submariners through the diving process.

All eyes were fixed upon the "Christmas tree" display, a series of
lights that showed whether numerous valves were open or closed.
The red lights quickly changed to green indicating that all valves
were closing normally.

The dive appeared to be going smoothly. Civilian observer Harold
Preble, a naval architect attached to Portsmouth, stood by, clocking the
dive. Lieutenant Doyle ordered the planesman to level off his horizon-
tal rudders at periscope depth, and Nake was already crouching at
the periscope. The depth gauge registered twenty-five feet . . .
thirty-five feet . . . forty feet . . . fifty feet . . . suddenly Yeoman
Charles Kuney turned to Lieutenant Naquin and shouted, "Engine
rooms are flooding, sir!"

The *Squalus* started sinking, stern first. The officers and men reacted immediately.

"Blow the main ballast!" shouted Naquin and Doyle together.

Doyle added, "Blow safety tanks! Blow bow buoyancy! Full power!"

Compressed air rushed into tanks, displacing the water that had just been taken in for the dive. The bow of the boat now rose twenty degrees, but the weight of the flooding compartments kept the *Squalus* from surfacing. The submarine hung in the water at about seventy feet for a few seconds and then started going down by the stern, the deck angling crazily to about forty degrees.

Hanging on to the periscope handles, Naquin had given the order to close all watertight hatches. Electrician's Mate Lloyd Maness struggled against the sharp angle to close the 300 pound hatch between the flooding aft battery compartment and the control room. Just as he almost had it closed, a voice cried out to open the hatch. Maness opened the hatch, and seven men tumbled to safety. Water was already coming into the control room as the submariner closed the hatch and dogged it down tight. Twenty-six men were on the other side of the hatch.

The depth gauge told of their plight as *Squalus* slipped down through the dark water: 100 feet . . . 150 . . . 185 . . . 200 . . . 225. Nake ordered his men to brace themselves for the jolt that would mean they had reached the ocean floor. Only the slightest of shudders announced that they had come to rest 242 feet below the surface. The deck angle decreased to about twelve degrees, making it a little easier to move about.

The after batteries had shorted out, and Chief Electrician's Mate Lawrence Gainer heroically leaped in among a shower of sparks and pulled the port and starboard switches in the forward battery compartment, thus preventing possible fires and explosions. His actions also plunged *Squalus* into total darkness. It was 8:45 A.M.

Nake went to work. Even though *Squalus* was his first major command, the officer was an experienced submariner. He had served in World War I–vintage subs, "O" and "R" boats, including R-14, stationed at Pearl Harbor. Most recently he had commanded S-46 and worked at the Navy Bureau of Engineering before being assigned as the first commanding officer of *Squalus*. No one had ever been rescued from a submarine at this depth before, but the Navy had been making tremendous strides in recovery methods in the last couple of years. In theory it was possible for the thirty-three survivors to be saved.

The skipper fired a red rocket, hoping to attract some passing vessel. He also released the telephone buoy, a yellowish-orange can with a brass plate that read: SUBMARINE SUNK HERE. U.S.S. SQUALUS. TELEPHONE INSIDE. Lieutenant Naquin divided the survivors into two parties. Lieutenant (j.g.) John Nichols, torpedo officer, was placed in charge of one group in the torpedo room, and Nake kept the rest in the control room.

With the temperature inside the sub plummeting, Nake faced a grim situation. With the exception of occasionally firing smoke rockets, there was little he and the others could do while they waited for a rescue party. He ordered blankets to be handed out, knowing the men must remain as warm as possible and keep quiet and calm.

"I wanted the men to sleep," Naquin was quoted years later in *Smithsonian*. "That way they'd avoid building up carbon dioxide, which will kill you if it reaches a concentration of seven percent." To avoid panic, Nake "accidentally" broke the sub's CO_2 test kit, thus making it impossible to judge the buildup of the poison.

When the *Squalus* didn't report surfacing, the officers at Portsmouth began to worry. Rear Admiral Cyrus W. Cole, the commandant, had made a mental note that *Squalus* should surface about 9:40. At 9:50, with no word from the submarine, he believed that something might have gone wrong. At 10:30, the admiral telephoned the Coast Guard station on the Isles of Shoals to check whether they had seen the submarine surface. They had not, of course, and Cole went into action, organizing a massive search effort.

Squalus's sister ship, *Sculpin* (SS-191) was dispatched, as was the rescue ship *Falcon*, stationed in New London, Connecticut. Unknown to those on board *Squalus*, the submarine's final radio message had been garbled, giving Portsmouth a false position to begin the search.

Forty fathoms down, in the chilly darkness, the men aboard *Squalus* waited. According to the log, red rockets were fired at 10:07, 10:24, and 11:40. At 12:23, the men chowed on pineapples, beans, tomatoes, and peaches. At 12:40 they fired another red rocket.

And then, at 12:55, far above sounded the screws of *Sculpin*. *Squalus* sent up another rocket, this one yellow, at 13:01. Five minutes later the submariners heard the heartening rattle of their sister sub's anchor chain.

At 1:21 p.m., telephone contact was established. Skipper of the *Sculpin*, Lieutenant Commander Warren Wilkin, got on the phone topside while Lieutenant Nichols hurriedly sketched the situation: two hundred forty-two feet down, main induction valve open, after compartments flooded, thirty-three known survivors.

Lieutenant Naquin got on the phone and said, "Hello, Wilkie," to which Wilkin replied, "Hello, Oliver," and the line went dead, snapped in two. Nake broke out a couple of four-pound sledge hammers and ordered the cork insulation stripped off part of the conning tower and in the forward torpedo room to enable men to bang on bare steel. The noise would help *Sculpin* locate them again. The men hammered out Morse code—one bang for a dot, two for a dash.

Meanwhile, the Navy tugs *Wandank* and *Penacook* arrived and began dragging for *Squalus*. At 7:30, the men on the sub heard a grapnel catch a deck railing. The *Penacook* had found them.

Nine long hours later, the rescue ship *Falcon* arrived. Squalus sent up another red rocket. Immediately, a message was relayed via *Falcon*'s oscillator: "Am mooring over you. Do not fire any more smoke bombs."

At 10:19 the next morning, more than twenty-five hours after the *Squalus* had gone down, the survivors heard the boots of a diver clumping about on the crippled sub's deck. Boatswain's Mate Martin Sibitsky, one of the Navy's most experienced divers, had been chosen as the first man to reach the sub. He worked quickly, not knowing how long he would have at this depth before deadly nitrogen narcosis might set in. Sibitsky made fast a haul-down wire to the escape hatch over the forward torpedo room before blacking out.

Miraculously, the diver was brought up safely—he regained full consciousness after stopping at his first decompression stage.

Now came the moment of truth. For the first time, a brand-new rescue chamber would be used in an attempt to rescue the stranded submariners. Designers Lieutenant Commander Charles Momsen and Commander Allan McCann were on hand to direct rescue operations. The pear-shaped McCann Rescue Chamber weighed nine tons, was ten feet high, and had a diameter of a little over seven feet. On its steel bottom was affixed a rubber gasket, five feet in diameter, which acted like a plumber's plunger when water was exploded from the lower of two compartments in the bell.

Divers William Badders and John Mihailowski lowered the McCann bell and secured it to the deck of *Squalus*. At about 12:30, the torpedo room hatch opened, letting in a flood of icy water. To the submariners' relief, a voice called out, "Hello, fellas, here we are." The speaker, Mihailowski, handed down hot coffee and soda lime to absorb the deadly CO_2. Fresh air pumped into the submarine through the McCann bell.

Naquin organized the men for escape. The weakest would go first, accompanied by civilian Preble and Lieutenant Nichols, who would brief those topside. In all, seven men left *Squalus* during the first lift. Each trip took about two hours. The next two trips lifted out nine men apiece, leaving Lieutenant Naquin and seven others to be rescued on the final trip.

A few minutes before 8 p.m., the McCann bell began its fourth and final ascent. Then, only ninety feet into its climb, the bell stopped. The cable had become frayed from usage, and the rescue chamber refused to budge. The divers in charge of the bell cracked jokes for the sake of the weary submariners, but master diver James McDonald quietly briefed Nake on the seriousness of their situation.

Aboard *Falcon*, Momsen and McCann rapidly went through their options and then ordered the divers to flood the ballast tanks and allow the bell to sink to the bottom. The bell drifted ponderously to the bottom and settled on the ocean floor. The ten men trapped in the bell could not get back into the submarine, and the cable could not lift them out. Once more, all Nake and his men could do was wait.

Another diver was sent down to unfasten the bad cable. He worked until, at the point of passing out, he finally severed the cable from the submarine. Two more divers went down, one at a time, to fasten a new, heavier cable to the top of the chamber. Both failed.

The chamber had been stalled for four hours, and time was running out. One risky option remained. Commander McCann passed down the order to diver McDonald, "Blow main ballast, thirty seconds!" McDonald turned a valve that forced compressed air into the ballast tanks for thirty seconds and stopped. Nothing happened.

"Blow fifteen seconds more," ordered McCann. Again, nothing.

McCann ordered another fifteen seconds, and, miraculously, the chamber responded, shuddering a little. On board *Falcon*, ten beefy seamen pulled on the light cable attached to the bell. And it began to rise.

At 12 a.m., Thursday, May 25, the rescue chamber broke the surface, ending a frightening ordeal for the thirty-three survivors of the *Squalus*. It also proved that it was possible to rescue men trapped at great depths, something that had never been done before. For his cool-headedness, Lieutenant Oliver F. Naquin was commended and cited for his "outstanding leadership."

The Navy salvaged *Squalus*, raising her in September 1939. The faulty main induction valve was fixed, and the boat was refitted and recommissioned as the *Sailfish*. She went on to a distinguished career during World War II, sinking seven ships. Nake eventually achieved the rank of admiral before retiring from the service.

Captain
Mad Jack
Percival

H E WAS GRUFF, a cantankerous cuss from Down East. Irascible, humorous, a superb seaman, patriotic. His name was John Percival, but to sailors around the world he was better known as Mad Jack.

Today he is mostly forgotten, but Mad Jack Percival stands in American naval history as a true hero, and it is Percival whom we can thank for saving America's oldest commissioned warship, the *U.S.S. Constitution*.

Born April 5, 1779, in West Barnstable, Massachusetts, Percival was the son of Captain John and Mary Snow Percival. Even at an early age, young John displayed the contrary nature that would earn him his curious epithet. According to local legend, one night he was served a supper of cornmeal mush while his parents dined on fish and potatoes. Viewing this as a grave injustice, the youth refused to eat. His father replied that he would be given nothing else until he had eaten the hasty pudding. True to his word, Captain Percival made sure that his son was served the same cold meal at breakfast.

That was enough of home life for John. He pulled on a clean shirt, grabbed a handful of his mother's biscuits, and struck out for Boston. Recounting the story in *Proceedings*, Allan Wescott wrote,

"Percival ran away from home and went to sea as a cabin boy and cook."

He was thirteen when he embarked on his long and colorful career at sea, and he rose through the ranks quickly, serving in the West Indian and transatlantic trade. It was in Lisbon, in 1797, while serving as second officer aboard *Thetis*, out of Boston, that Percival was seized by a British press gang and forced into the Royal Navy.

The first British warship he served aboard was *H.M.S. Victory*, the flagship of Sir John Jervis. According to family tradition, Percival served under Nelson aboard the *Victory* at Trafalgar in 1805. In truth, he escaped from the British while in port in Madeira in 1799, rowing several miles in a stolen ship's boat to the American vessel *Washington*.

During the naval conflict between the United States and France, Percival served as master's mate aboard the warship *Delaware*. He was warranted as a midshipman in 1800, at the age of twenty-one, and discharged the following year when peace was established.

Percival returned to the merchant marine, serving as both mate and master for several years. Legend has it that on one cruise, virtually all of the crew died of yellow fever. The only survivors were Percival and the ship's dog. When rescued off the coast of Pernambuco, Percival was thrown into prison on suspicion of piracy. Another time, about 1805, he found himself imprisoned and robbed of his ship at Santa Cruz, Tenerife.

In 1809, Percival rejoined the U.S. Navy as a sailing master. Stationed in the blockaded harbor of New York during the War of 1812, Percival pulled a daring attack that earned him a favorable reputation and bolstered his career. During a band concert at New York's Battery Park on July 5, 1813, Percival rounded up a crew of thirty-two sailors. Outlining his plan, Percival instructed the men to gather up as much stale fruit and vegetables as they could find in the Fly Market district. When the sailors returned to the wharf, Percival was waiting with a decrepit fisherman's smack named the *Yankee*. The produce was arranged on deck, and Percival added a goat, a pair of sheep, a crate of ducks, and a goose to his cargo. The sailors were packed below, fully armed.

Percival, wearing a farmer's jacket and straw hat, worked the boat out into the harbor. About three miles out, the *Yankee* was overtaken by the British tender *Eagle*, carrying a complement of thirteen soldiers.

The master of the *Eagle* hailed Percival and told him to bring his produce to the British flagship. Instead, the American spun his helm hard against the tender. At the given signal, the sailors came tumbling out of the little vessel's hold and quickly overpowered the British. Two hours later, the *Yankee* arrived at the Battery with the *Eagle* in tow. Percival was received as a hero.

Later, as sailing master of the sloop of war *Peacock*, Percival participated in three highly successful cruises, capturing seventeen enemy vessels worth more than $1 million. *Peacock*'s commander, Captain Lewis Warrington, wrote of Percival that he handled his craft when engaged with the enemy "as if he had been working her into a roadstead."

For his heroism in the capture of the British brig *Epervier*, Sailing Master Percival was given a sword by Congress and received a vote of thanks by his hometown. Captain Warrington recommended Percival's promotion to lieutenant in 1814.

In 1821, Percival served as lieutenant commander aboard the *Porpoise*, which was engaged in capturing pirate ships that preyed on American vessels. For his deeds, several Boston insurance companies presented Commander Percival with a service of silver plate. Two years later, Mad Jack, as the eligible bachelor had come to be known, married Maria Pinkerton of Trenton, New Jersey.

Also in 1821, Percival served as first lieutenant in Commodore Isaac Hull's flagship, *United States*, in the Pacific. In 1826, Percival commanded the twelve-gun schooner *Dolphin* and conducted the search for the mutineers of the whaleship *Globe*. The *Dolphin* was the first American warship ever to visit Hawaii, where Percival rendered valuable service in protecting American interests and helped salvage cargo and money from the shipwrecked *London*.

While Percival disagreed with American missionaries over their anti-prostitution ordinances in Hawaii, he also successfully ended a sailors' riot against the restrictions. Several of the crew had to be

Captain John "Mad Jack" Percival, a few months before his death in 1862. OFFICIAL U.S. NAVY PHOTO-GRAPH.

placed in irons, and the chief missionary was invited aboard to witness the subsequent floggings.

Percival was promoted to full commander in 1831 and skippered the *U.S.S. Cyane* in the Mediterranean in 1838 and 1839. In 1841, he was promoted to captain and stationed at Norfolk, Virginia.

Also stationed at Norfolk, was the aging *U.S.S. Constitution*, "Old Ironsides," which presented a problem to the Navy. She was the most historic vessel in the fleet, but it was questionable whether she could be salvaged. The secretary of the Navy had estimated the cost of restoration at $150,000, a price considered too high by the government.

Mad Jack went to work to save the beloved *Constitution*. He asked the authorities if he could have a look at the frigate and give them a second opinion. Upon receiving permission, Captain Percival went directly to the docks. The sixty-two-year-old officer stripped off his jacket and trousers and, clad only in his underwear, dived into the water.

Percival personally saved "Old Ironsides," today the oldest commissioned warship in the U.S. Navy.

Percival swam around the warship, poking at her timbers with an awl. Then he came topside, pulled on his trousers, and climbed into the rigging, inspecting shrouds, stays, lifts, and braces. Finally, he climbed down and returned to the secretary's office. He asked for $10,000 and a competent crew of ship riggers. Not only could he restore Old Ironsides, Percival proclaimed, he could make her fit to sail around the world.

For the next two years, Captain Percival carefully supervised the repairs to the *Constitution*. By 1843, the work was complete, and Mad Jack was made commanding officer of the frigate. True to his word, the captain proceeded to take the old girl on a round-the-world cruise.

The *Constitution* sailed for Africa, rounded the Cape of Good Hope, and returned to America by way of China, Hawaii, and California. Covering some 55,000 miles and calling at twenty-six ports, the cruise of Old Ironsides was to be Captain Mad Jack Percival's last sea command, but it was a great one.

During the voyage, the *Constitution* captured a pirate ship in the Indian Ocean, freeing the captive Imam of Muscat. The Imam had been making his annual passage to Zanzibar, where he was sultan, when taken prisoner by pirates. To show his appreciation to Captain Percival, the Arabian leader presented Mad Jack with a richly jeweled sword. Later, while passing through the Bay of Bengal, the frigate rescued Bishop Dominique Lefevre of Isampolis from the King of Cochin.

The *Constitution* returned to America in 1846, her future assured because of Captain Percival's efforts. In 1855, the captain's name was placed on the reserve list, and Mad Jack returned to his native Massachusetts and took up residence in Dorchester. He died seven years later, on September 17, 1862, at the age of eighty-three.

Contemporary accounts eulogized the flamboyant officer as "brave, kind-hearted, generous, patriotic, and faithful." Though his temper gave him his nickname, Mad Jack Percival was also known as a seaman of extraordinarily sound judgment, a man of iron will and fearlessness, loved by his crewmen.

George
Tilton's
Long Hike
for Help

T HE WHALING SHIP *Belvedere* lay helpless in the Arctic ice. Her men, along with the crews of the destroyed whaleships *Orca* and *Freeman*, had spent eight days traversing the dangerous ice to reach the relative safety of Sea Horse Island. It was September 1897, and the stranded whalemen figured that they had enough provisions to last until the first of July.

It had been a harsh season, the iciest anyone could recall. The whales had been sparse, the seas rough, the cold early. One ship of the North Pacific whaling fleet, the *Navarch*, had been trapped in the ice and had drifted away to the northwest with all hands on board.

Both the *Orca* and the *Freeman* had been crushed by the ice, but not before their crews had escaped to the *Belvedere*, which had been trying to make her way to Point Barrow, Alaska. The 150 men who were now encamped on the island faced an uncertain future.

George Fred Tilton, third mate of the *Belvedere*, approached the three captains with a plan. He would travel overland and send help. The captains were doubtful of Tilton's ability to succeed but agreed to let him try.

For companions, Tilton picked two Siberian natives and a team of eight sled dogs. A special sled fitted with a small sail was designed, some provisions gathered, and Tilton and his party set off on an epic journey.

The first stop was at the trapped *Belvedere*. Tilton retrieved a compass and other navigating instruments, a chart, and guns and ammunition. The little party began its trek on October 31. By the next day they had traveled twenty-five miles, but a blizzard halted further travel until November 3. The next two days took the men across treacherous mountains. The sled and dogs had to be hauled across peaks and crevasses. Tilton decided to abandon the high ground in favor of the easier but longer route hugging the coastline. Upon reaching level terrain, the party gave themselves a much needed three-day rest.

A raging snowstorm soon halted the travelers on November 8, and they were forced to construct a snow shelter for protection. The next morning they continued and by midnight reached an Indian village, where they traded cartridges and powder for some seal meat.

The next leg of the journey provided the most trying conditions for the party, a stretch of fifteen miles of sharp rises and drops. Again, the dogs and sled had to be raised and lowered by rope, one at a time. Three days later the men found themselves at a seemingly insurmountable impasse. Before them lay a river 150 feet wide, with no means of crossing. To retrace their steps was impossible. To make matters worse, they were also out of food.

Tilton made a bold decision. He began hewing at the ice with his snow saw and, working all day, fashioned a crude raft large enough for the men and dogs to attempt a crossing. Their luck held, and they managed to get across the river. They had now gone without food for four days.

The next morning, the group was blessed by finding a flock of ducks and the carcass of a whale. The Indians and dogs gorged on whale meat while Tilton built a fire and dined on roast duck. The whaleman reckoned his position to be eighteen miles from the whaling station at Point Hope. Despite a blinding blizzard, Tilton ordered the journey to resume after their feast.

Leaving the dogs, sled, and gear with the whale carcass, Tilton tied himself and his two companions together and forged ahead along the coast. The men could see nothing as they traveled. Occasionally, Tilton would check his position by digging through the snow to see if he had strayed out over the water. If he struck dirt, he knew he was still on land. If he found only ice, he corrected their course.

At one point, when Tilton figured he was about a mile from the station, the Indians gave up and lay down. The whaleman forced them back on their feet and trudged ahead. The snow was swirling so thickly that Tilton literally bumped into the wall of the whaling station. By feeling along its side, he found the door and walked in.

A Norwegian whaleman, named Anderson, jumped up in fright and asked, "For God's sake, where did you come from?" The Indians lay down on the floor and slept while Tilton accepted coffee

Whaleman George Tilton undertook an arduous journey to bring help to the marooned survivors of the whaleship Belvedere.

and hardtack and told his story to Anderson. The three men rested for a couple of days before returning to Cape Lisburne, where they had left the dogs and gear. All but one of the dogs were there. They later found the other dog, which had apparently been blown over a cliff by high winds.

Tilton recruited two new traveling companions and three new dogs and, on November 29, once again set out on his mission. In March, he abandoned the sled and continued southward, sending messages by way of boat owners about the plight of the men trapped in the Arctic.

By the end of his journey, George Tilton had covered about three thousand miles, mostly on foot. He had averaged eleven miles a day for about nine months. The famous U.S. Coast Guard Cutter *Bear* was dispatched to Point Barrow and the stranded whalemen were rescued.

Five years later, Tilton returned to the Arctic, this time as captain of the *Belvedere*. In later years, Captain Tilton delighted thousands of tourists visiting the *Charles W. Morgan* in Mystic Seaport with tales of his heroic walk and other whaling adventures.

The Loss
of Lord
Kitchener

W HEN *Kapitänleutnant* Kurt Beitzon and the crew of *U-75* sowed the submarine's cargo of mines around Scapa Flow in late May 1916, the German officer had no idea of the impending magnitude of his actions. One of those mines would strike a raw nerve in the British people and cast a shroud of mystery that remains intact today.

Horatio Herbert, Lord Kitchener, Earl of Khartoum, had led a charmed life. Born in County Kerry, Ireland, in 1850, Kitchener was commissioned an officer in the Royal Engineers in 1871. In a time when the British Army was looked upon as an assortment of amateurs, Kitchener worked to bring professionalism to the service. His sense of duty and hard work led to his subsequent meteoric rise through the ranks.

He served with distinction on the outposts of the British Empire, becoming Governor of Suakin, commander-in-chief of the Egyptian Army, and conqueror of the Sudan. Kitchener's daring exploits thrilled the citizens of the United Kingdom, and in 1898, he was rewarded by Queen Victoria by being admitted into the nobility.

After service as Governor General of the Sudan, Lord Kitchener was sent to South Africa to quell the Boers. Victorious, he returned to England and was made a viscount. The next assignment found Kitchener as commander-in-chief of India, where he quarreled with the British Viceroy, Lord Curzon. Kitchener's tremendous popularity at home ensured that he got his way, and he more or less ruled India until 1911 when he was dispatched to govern Egypt and the Sudan. His ultimate plan of uniting Egypt, the Sudan, Kenya, and Uganda into a new Eastern Viceroyalty was interrupted by the outbreak of the Great War. With much reluctance, Kitchener, by now an earl, accepted the position of secretary of state for war.

With typical bluntness, Lord Kitchener dismissed the British Territorial Army as hopeless and the regular Army as not much better. He foresaw the atrocities of the "War to End All Wars" and laughed at his cabinet fellows who proclaimed that the war would be over in a matter of weeks. Kitchener personally set about building a massive volunteer army, convinced that the only way England could emerge victorious was to throw millions of men into the effort.

Kitchener's portrait appeared on recruiting posters, and men flocked to sign up. Future Prime Minister David Lloyd George, then minister of munitions, wrote later, "I doubt whether any other man could at that moment have attracted the hundreds of thousands who rallied to the flag at his appearance." If he offended the ruling professional politicians, Lord Kitchener was still easily the man admired most by the British citizenry.

The earl was used to doing as he pleased. After all, he had ruled larger nations than England, and it rankled him to have to comply with political niceties and procedures. Never one to delegate responsibility, Lord Kitchener worked tirelessly to build up Britain's industries for the impending horror and attempted to oversee every aspect of the British military. Critics have charged that he wasted his own efforts and hampered those of others by his autocratic rule, but no one could or can fault him for the energy and good intentions he invested in his work.

On May 13, 1916, Lord Kitchener received a personal invitation from Czar Nicholas II to visit Russia. The war was going badly for the Russians, and Nicholas had made himself commander-in-chief

Lord Kitchener was so popular that his image was used on British recruiting posters in World War I.

after a string of disastrous defeats. It was his hope that the well-known and well-respected Kitchener could rally the troops in Russia while supplying military expertise, war materiel, and financial assistance to the beleaguered nation.

The offer came at a good time, since Secretary for War Lord Kitchener found himself increasingly under attack by the Liberals in Parliament. On Friday, May 26, his Lordship agreed to undertake the mission. He had no way of knowing that the German U-boat that held his fate had departed for the cold waters of Scotland on the previous Saturday. *U-75* arrived off the Orkneys on May 28 and began laying her mines.

The Admiralty went about planning his trip. Although the mission was supposedly a secret, there is evidence that a number of people in and outside the government were aware of it. A message was sent to Admiral Sir John Jellicoe, commander, British Grand Fleet, to detail a warship to convey Lord Kitchener to the Russian port of Archangel.

Jellicoe and his staff very quickly found themselves engaged in a more pressing issue, the Battle of Jutland, the only major sea battle of the war. Even as Lord Kitchener posted an invitation on May 31 to members of Parliament to join him in his office on Friday, June 2, the British Grand Fleet and the German High Seas Fleet were brawling in the North Sea.

The casualties were enormous: lost were fourteen Royal Navy vessels and 6,000 British officers and men; eleven German warships and about 3,000 sailors. While the German Navy had inflicted the greater punishment, it retired to safe harbors, never again to venture forth in force during the war.

It was under the pall of such heavy casualties that Lord Kitchener met with those members responding to his invitation. What had been planned as a conciliatory farewell meeting with a few disgruntled politicians in the war secretary's office turned into a major political event in the House of Commons.

In a packed committee room, the formidable Earl of Khartoum, hero of the Sudan, set forth a defense of his work as secretary of state for war. An enthralled audience forgot its grievances with this rigid Conservative and interrupted repeatedly with applause. Ironically, this was the last victory Lord Kitchener was ever to enjoy. He left Parliament in good humor and went first to Number 10 Downing Street to meet with Prime Minister Herbert Asquith and then to Buckingham Palace to chat with his close friend, the King. After another briefing with the King the following day, Kitchener retired to his country home for the remainder of the day. Sunday found him at work in his office. After dinner, his Lordship and his party gathered at King's Cross station to begin the journey northward.

On board a special four-coach train were Lord Kitchener; his longtime friend and secretary, Colonel Oswald FitzGerald; H. J. O'Bierne, Counselor at the British embassy at Petrograd; technical advisors Sir Frederick Donaldson and L. S. Robertson; Brigadier W. Ellershaw; Lieutenant R. D. Macpherson; Scotland Yard Detective Sergeant McLaughlin; and three servants—a total of eleven.

At Thurso, Scotland, the next morning the weather was harsh. Strong winds buffeted the party, and stinging rain swept across the pierside station. If the weather bothered Lord Kitchener, he gave no indication. The delegation boarded the destroyer *H.M.S. Oak* which transported them to Admiral Jellicoe's flagship, the *Iron Duke*.

Secrecy of the secretary's visit had been kept at that end, and the arrival of such a well-known face caused much excitement aboard the warship. Wearing a heavy wool field marshal's overcoat, Lord Kitchener joined Jellicoe for a tour of the dreadnought. Afterward, he joined his host for lunch, expressing that he was looking forward to his passage to Russia as "a real holiday." He added that he was most eager to get underway.

At 4:14 P.M. on Monday, the Kitchener party departed the *Iron Duke* to be piped aboard the cruiser *H.M.S. Hampshire*, Captain Herbert Savill commanding. Savill had learned of his distinguished guest's impending visit only a few hours earlier, and provisions had not yet been made for Kitchener and his attendants.

The weather steadily worsened. Admiral Jellicoe and his staff then made the fateful decision: the *Hampshire* should proceed through the western channel from Scapa Flow instead of the usual eastern channel because of weather conditions. The channel had not been swept for mines in at least "three days," according to the admiral. In fact, *U-75* had sown its deadly mines in the channel a full week before, but Jellicoe and his senior officers were confident that the western channel was unobstructed.

At 4:45, the *Hampshire*, accompanied by the destroyers *Victor* and *Unity*, steamed for open water. Once at sea, it was discovered that the gale had changed direction. The western channel offered no protection from the fifty-knot winds, and by 6:30, both the *Victor* and the *Unity* had been dismissed from escort duty because of severe weather.

An hour later, even the mighty cruiser had slowed considerably against the mountainous waves. Rounding the Orkneys, the *Hampshire* stood a mile and a half offshore of Marwick Head.

At 7:40 P.M. a terrific explosion rumbled through the warship, knocking out all lights. Immediately, the vessel heeled over and began sinking by the bow.

On shore, an observer with the Orkney Royal Garrison Artillery had witnessed the explosion, and he hurried to telegraph for help.

On board, orders were given to abandon ship. Lifeboats were lowered into the water only to be smashed to pieces by the churning waves. Reports later placed Lord Kitchener in a variety of places: in his cabin, near the lifeboats, standing boldly on the quarterdeck.

The combination of fierce weather and bitterly cold water made the odds of surviving the sinking remote. The ship sank quickly, completely disappearing in less than fifteen minutes. Despite the fact that every available vessel was dispatched to aid the *Hampshire*, only twelve men were rescued. Not one officer or member of Kitchener's party was among that small number.

The effect on the British people is hard to imagine. For an American of the period it would have been comparable to learning that James Montgomery Flagg's "Uncle Sam" had been killed, with the exception that Lord Kitchener was a real person, albeit larger than life. England went into a time of mourning. Lloyd George described it, "A pall of dismay descended on the spirit of the people. . . . The news of a defeat could not have produced such a sense of irreparable disaster."

Almost immediately, the press theorized about betrayal and espionage. Headlines warned of German spies in London. Even stranger were the rumors that sprang to life: Kitchener had been captured by the Germans; he had been taken to a mysterious cave in the Hebrides where he lay in a trance. Questions were raised as to why the *Hampshire* had not radioed for help. Why had the Navy not reacted to the catastrophe sooner? Who had betrayed Lord Kitchener? Who had killed him? Had the corrupt court in Russia revealed the secret mission? Had the Germans lain in wait off the Orkneys?

Lord Kitchener's close friend and first biographer, Sir George Arthur, intimated that he had been offered a look at the official Navy records on the sinking of the *Hampshire* if he would swear not to reveal the Admiralty's findings. The Admiralty refused to publish the so-called "secret report," despite an inquiry by the House of Commons.

Elaborate theories were put forth during the following years as to how and why the Earl of Khartoum was killed. Books and movies claimed to have unraveled the mystery, even naming names of alleged spies involved in the plot.

In 1926, a full decade after the tragedy, the Admiralty issued a white paper about the loss of the *Hampshire*, but it was heavily censored and left many questions unanswered. Its defensive tone dissatisfied many. The official findings have yet to be released.

The most likely explanation is that the loss of *H.M.S. Hampshire* and Lord Kitchener was merely a misfortune of war. The sowing of mines was a routine practice for German submarines. According to German documents, *U-75* left on its mission before Lord Kitchener even conveyed his response to the Czar.

That the less-frequented western channel from Scapa Flow was mined has been attributed to poor intelligence on the part of the German Admiralty. That the *Hampshire* was ordered through that channel perhaps reflected poor judgment—certainly not an intentional death sentence. Rescue operations were mounted as soon as possible, but the severe weather made successful sea rescue impossible. Had the weather been calm, it is probable that most of the crew and possibly Lord Kitchener himself could have been saved.

What is more interesting to consider is what might have happened if the secretary for war had been successful in his mission. Would the great soldier have been able to boost the sagging morale of the Russian troops? Could he have mapped a strategy that would have bought the Czarist regime more time? According to Admiral Sir John Jellicoe, Lord Kitchener, in speaking of his mission to

Russia, said he was not "very sanguine" that he could achieve much during the visit.

If, however, he had been successful, it is possible that the outcome of history would have been quite different indeed. Without the continued crushing defeats suffered during the war, perhaps there would have been no successful Bolshevik Revolution. And without a Communist victory, hundreds of millions of people might have been spared the more than seventy years of totalitarian rule that was to follow.

The
Texas
Navy

R ETURNING FROM Texas aboard the schooner *San Felipe* following eighteen months of imprisonment in Mexico, Stephen Austin held little hope for peace. As the sound of shots boomed across the water, whatever hope might have remained quickly evaporated.

Ahead lay the Mexican Revenue Cutter *Correro*, firing upon a small Texas vessel. As the *San Felipe* approached the action, the *Correro* heeled about and, without warning, fired upon the newcomer. The *San Felipe*'s skipper, Captain W. A. Hurd, ordered his men to return fire. The war for Texan independence had begun.

A classic naval duel ensued, with the *Correro* finally surrendering to the Texas ship. The two set a course for New Orleans, where the battle continued in court. The judge eventually threw out the case, but Mexican General Antonio Lopez de Santa Ana now had the excuse he had been looking for to send troops into Texas.

When most people think about the war between Texas and Mexico, they tend to remember the Alamo, armies marching across dusty plains, and the Texas Rangers shooting it out with invading hordes, but a strong case can be made that much of the credit for the republic's independence should go to the little-known Texas Navy.

Recognizing the importance of a naval force in the Gulf, one of the first actions undertaken by the Texas Council was the authorization of a Texas Navy and letters of marque for privateers in November 1835. Sea lanes between New Orleans and Texas had to be kept open to allow the unrestricted flow of supplies and volunteers. Austin relinquished his command and traveled to the United States to raise funds, in part to purchase a navy.

Almost immediately, the privateer *William Robbins* captured the Mexican warship *Bravo*, but because the public held privateers in low regard, the Texas government bought the *William Robbins* and rechristened her the *Liberty*. She put to sea again with the same captain and crew.

The Texas Navy soon consisted of four schooners, including the 125-ton *Independence* (formerly the U.S. Revenue Cutter *Samuel D. Ingham*), captained by Commodore William Brown; the sixty-ton *Liberty*, commanded by Captain Jeremiah Brown; the 125-ton *Invincible*, commanded by Captain C. E. Hawkins; the 125-ton *Brutus*, commanded by Captain William Hard; and the armed raider *Flash*, under the command of Captain Luke Flavel. The privateers *Thomas*, *Toby*, and *Terrible* rounded out the fleet.

In January, Santa Ana began his invasion, secure in his belief that the Mexican Navy could supply his army of 6,000. He intended to return to Mexico by sea, following the defeat of the Texans.

Resupply by sea was essential to the Mexican Army because its bases were cut off from the rest of the country by the "Desert of Dead Horses," an unforgiving, inhospitable stretch of arid land. Despite pleas by his officers, including General Vicente Filisola, to strengthen the small Mexican Navy, Santa Ana, who often likened himself to Napoleon, did nothing to augment his navy, and his soldiers began their march with too few provisions.

The Texas Navy quickly became a presence to be reckoned with in the Gulf. Every ship in the fledgling navy took cargoes bound for the Mexican Army. To combat her losses, Mexico began shipping supplies under false manifests that indicated the cargoes were bound for New Orleans. The Texan sailors, however, maintained that any

Mexican cargo constituted fair game, war materiel or not, regardless of its destination.

Despite his success at the Alamo, Santa Ana had lost a considerable number of men. Now, the bulk of his supplies had been intercepted by the Texans. In Mexico, Vice President Miguel Barragan had died on March 1, 1836, and Santa Ana feared that he would lose the presidency to Acting President Jose Justo Corro. Accordingly, the besieged Mexican leader made secret arrangements with a German schooner to pick him up on the night of April 19 and take him to the waiting *Bravo*, which, in turn, would ferry him back to Mexico.

On March 3, the *Liberty* attacked and captured the Mexican schooner *Pelicano* at Sisal. Captain Brown discovered that the *Pelicano* carried a cargo of rifles and ammunition, and these much-needed supplies now went to General Sam Houston and his men. On April 3, the *Invincible* attacked the Mexican troop and supply ship *Bravo*, capturing it and the American vessel *Pocket*, which also carried supplies for the Mexican Army.

Elsewhere in the Gulf, the action was much the same. Texan ships ran down Mexican vessels and diverted their precious supplies to the Texas Army. Within a matter of weeks, the Texas Navy had gained the upper hand in the Gulf.

Texas averted a tragedy when President David Burnet narrowly escaped the Mexican Army at Harrisburg. Burnet and members of his cabinet fled aboard the *Flash*.

Santa Ana torched the city but could not understand where his resupply ships might be. As it turned out, he had arrived for his rendezvous with the German vessel just in time to see the Texas Navy in action. As the horrified Mexican leader looked on, the schooner was burned. He had lost his means of escape. Two days later came the Battle of San Jacinto, the defeat of the Mexican Army, and the imprisonment of Santa Ana by Sam Houston.

At sea, the war continued to rage, the navies unaware that the land action was over. Two months after San Jacinto, the Mexican schooner *Watchman* arrived at the Texas port of Copano. Major I. W. Burton and about thirty Texas Ranges saw the ship and signaled her. Aboard the *Watchman*, the Texas colors were run up; Burton's men did not respond. Nor did they respond when the ship ran up the U.S. flag. Finally, the Mexican ensign was raised, at which point Burton ordered his men to cheer loudly.

A boat dispatched by the *Watchman* was quickly captured by Burton and his "horse marines," much to the surprise of the Mexicans. The Texans rowed out to the ship and took it as well. The Rangers then commandeered the *Watchman* and soon captured two more schooners, the *Comanche* and the *Fanny Butler*. In all, Burton's horse marines captured $25,000 worth of supplies.

Searching for the three missing schooners, the Mexican brig *Vencedor del Alamo* encountered the *Brutus* at anchor at Galveston and moved in for the kill. Quick-thinking citizens towed the *Brutus* out to deeper water where she would be able to maneuver. The Mexican ship fled, with the *Brutus* trailing her to Vera Cruz. A one-ship blockade ensued, but none of the Mexican ships would venture out of port for a fight.

At the end of the summer, the Texas Navy was recalled for repairs. The *Invincible* and *Brutus* went to New York. The *Liberty* put in at New Orleans and was promptly seized and auctioned off for sums due by the Republic of Texas. The *Independence* lay docked in New Orleans, idle since the death of her captain.

Despite additional funding from the Texas Congress, the navy had fallen on hard times. Returning from New York and capturing six Mexican vessels, the *Invincible* and *Brutus* were grounded and destroyed in a storm. To Texas's great embarrassment, the *Independence* was captured by the *Vencedor del Alamo* as she returned from Washington with Texas Commissioner William Wharton on board. Wharton was jailed in Matamoros, and the *Independence* absorbed into the Mexican Navy.

Mexico, in the meantime, became engaged in a war with France, giving Texas time to rebuild its navy. Eight new ships were on order by the time Houston was completing his first three-year term as president.

Mirabeau Lamar, former vice president and newly elected president, held great dreams for Texas, envisioning a permanent republic that would stretch from the Gulf Coast to the Pacific. Integral to that success would be a strong navy.

The $800,000 fleet, delivered in 1839 and 1840, consisted of the eight-gun steamer *Zavala*; the twenty-gun, 600-ton sloop-of-war *Austin*; the 300-ton brigs *Wharton* and *Archer*; and the 170-ton schooners *San Bernard*, *San Antonio*, and *San Jacinto*. Lamar chose as his new commanding officer twenty-nine-year-old Edwin Moore, who had been a lieutenant in the U.S. Navy. The adventurous Moore accepted the rank of post captain commanding, more commonly referred to as commodore, at the salary of $200 per month.

It has been written that Texas had everything it needed to be a nation—plenty of land, a hearty citizenry, an army and navy, politi-

Lieutenant Edwin Moore, formerly of the U.S. Navy, led the Texas Navy to victory in the republic's bid for independence.

cians, a constitution, customs agents—everything except money. The coffers were dreadfully low, and the Texas Navy soon came to be viewed as a revenue-generating operation.

The fleet sailed in June 1840, while President Lamar attempted to hold diplomatic negotiations with Mexico through Texas envoy James Treat. When the talks failed, Lamar authorized Commodore Moore and the navy to take prizes. Moore also arranged an alliance with the independence-minded Mexican state of Yucatan, promising protection to Yucatecan ports for the price of $8,000 per month.

Commodore Moore sailed on December 13, 1841, the last day of Lamar's administration. The Texas vessels wreaked havoc with Mexican shipping, taking cargoes and destroying ships. Moore captured the Tabascan town of San Juan Bautista and levied a war fine of $25,000.

Following his inauguration as President, Sam Houston issued an order stating "that the squadron under your command return forthwith to the port of Galveston, and there await further orders." That order did not reach the commodore until four months later.

In March 1842, Mexico once again invaded Texas, taking the town of San Antonio. President Houston ordered the Texas Navy to blockade Mexico but conveniently supplied no funds for this undertaking.

Moore now sailed to New Orleans for refitting. The *San Bernard* was wrecked off Galveston, and the *San Antonio* disappeared (she was later reported in the Caribbean, flying a pirate flag). The navy arrived in New Orleans two vessels short, with empty stores and no money to pay off the crews. The warships lay in the yards, unable to sail until payment could be made. Houston, meanwhile, had begun reducing the republic's expenses. Excluding a few companies of Texas Rangers, the army was sent home, officials' salaries were slashed, and in January 1843, Congress secretly voted to sell the Texas Navy.

Unaware of his adopted country's decision, Commodore Moore had renewed negotiations with Don Martin Peraza of the Yucatan. In February, Peraza arrived in New Orleans with cash to pay for the navy's repair bills and a contract for services at the original price of $8,000 per month.

Houston sent three Texas agents to New Orleans just before the navy was to sail to advise Moore of his decision to abolish the Texas Navy. The commodore proved to be a persuasive man, however, and one of the agents, Colonel James Morgan, actually joined him on the cruise to the Yucatan.

The fleet set sail April 19, 1843. Houston was furious and charged Commodore Moore and his men with "disobedience, contumacy, and mutiny." Off the coast of the Yucatan, Moore was too busy to worry about politics back home. On April 30, off Campeche, the Texas Navy attacked the blockading Mexican squadron which included two brigs, two schooners, the armed steamer *Regenerador*, and several Mexican ironclads.

On May 16 the navy again attacked the Mexican fleet, inflicting great damage to the ironclads and disabling the warships *Guadalupe* and *Montezuma*. Casualties to the Texan fleet included five dead. The Mexicans suffered losses of eighty-seven men.

The Mexicans had been routed, and the threat of an invasion of Texas by sea no longer existed. Just as the war with Mexico had begun at sea, so, too, it now ended at sea. The action off the Yucatan proved to be the final battle before the United States annexed Texas.

Commodore Moore received President Houston's proclamation relieving him of command on June 1, 1843, and immediately set sail for Galveston. He and the men of the Texas Navy were welcomed as heroes upon their arrival. The sheriff of Galveston ignored his orders to arrest Moore, and the citizens began planning formal balls in honor of their navy officers and men. Moore wrote to the Texas Department of Navy, demanding a trial.

The government handed Moore a dishonorable discharge and a list of twenty-two criminal charges, including murder. In a show of loyalty to their commanding officer, none of Moore's junior officers would accept command of the navy, and the responsibility finally fell to Sailing Master Daniel Lloyd.

Congress agreed to grant Moore a trial. Five months later, a joint committee of the Texas House and Senate exculpated him of all charges. Furthermore, the commodore was commended for his actions. Eight months after that, a three-month-long court-martial found Commodore Moore guilty of four minor infractions. The verdict was handed down two days before Houston left office. It was the end, effectively, of the Texas Navy.

The Republic of Texas was annexed by the United States in 1845 as the twenty-eighth state, fulfilling the desires of many of those who had engineered the Texas Revolution.

Nelson's
First Taste
of
Glory

VICE ADMIRAL LORD Horatio Nelson, Duke of Bronte, Viscount of the Nile and Burnham Thorpe, Knight of the Bath, remains one of England's most celebrated heroes. He is remembered for his stunning victories at Trafalgar and the Battle of the Nile, as well as for his torrid love affair with the beautiful Lady Emma Hamilton.

Despite his early rapid promotions and his later achievement of fame and glory, Nelson's middle years proved frustrating, and his future looked uncertain at best.

Born the son of a country rector in 1758, at Burnham Thorpe, Horatio Nelson went to sea as a midshipman at the age of twelve, under the patronage of a wealthy and well-connected uncle, Captain Maurice Suckling. He passed his examination for lieutenant early and was promoted at eighteen. His outstanding service in the West Indies led to promotion to commander eighteen months later. In June 1779, he became a captain at the age of twenty.

Captain Nelson conducted various operations in the West Indies, including an expedition deep into Nicaragua. He commanded several vessels and served as an aide-de-camp to Prince William Henry, future King of England. At the prince's urging, the young captain married Francis "Fanny" Nisbet, the widowed niece of the Governor of Nevis, in 1787.

Following his wedding, Captain Nelson and his bride returned to England where, as an officer without a ship, he was put on half pay. Nelson had been making a name for himself in the West Indies but had fallen into disfavor with powerful merchants who sought to conduct illegal trade with the United States.

For his scrupulous honesty and his desire to enforce the law in the Caribbean, Captain Nelson now found himself out of work and embroiled in litigation with traders and American merchant captains. At a time that should have been his prime, Nelson idly strolled the walks of Norfolk and tended his father's garden.

Repeated entreaties to the Admiralty, including officers who had once looked favorably upon him, went unheeded, and Nelson languished in the English countryside between the ages of twenty-nine and thirty-four.

The French Revolution, along with the export of its radical ideas to the heart of England, stirred the British Admiralty into action. Captain Nelson was recalled to duty five days after the execution of King Louis XVI of France. Six days later, on February 1, 1793, France declared war on England.

When Nelson reported to his new command, it was the first time he had stepped foot on a Royal Navy warship in more than five years. He was thrilled. As commander of *H.M.S. Agamemnon*, Nelson sailed for the Mediterranean, serving under his old friend, Lord Hood—the same Lord Hood who had ignored his pleas to the Admiralty.

Following the surrender of Toulon, which the *Agamemnon* had been blockading, Nelson was dispatched to Naples on a diplomatic mission to the King and Queen of the Kingdom of the Two Sicilies. It was here that he met Lady Emma Hamilton, wife of British Ambassador Sir William Hamilton.

Sir William offered his assistance to Nelson and, together with Sir John Acton, the Neapolitan prime minister, they approached King Ferdinand with a plea for reinforcements to occupy Toulon.

Lord Nelson is regarded as England's greatest naval hero.

The King agreed and provided a force of 4,000 troops. Despite the reinforcements, however, the city would fall again to the French.

Nelson now sailed for Corsica and established a blockade. After inspecting the island and its defenses, the captain of the *Agamemnon* recommended storming the fortress of Bastia. Lord Hood eventually agreed, and Nelson set about preparing the siege. Heavy cannon were taken ashore and dragged on sledges along inhospitable terrain.

Remarkably, the fortress fell, due mainly to the blockade and subsequent shortage of food. Some 4,500 French troops surrendered to about 1,000 English troops. Captain Nelson's high spirits were dashed, however, when he learned that Lord Hood gave him little credit for his actions in the official report to the Admiralty.

Nelson was more determined than ever to win recognition as he sailed for Corsica's other principal fortress at Calvi. Calvi would prove more difficult—the only available landing and staging area was less than ideal, situated more than three miles from the citadel.

Sailors once more engineered crude roads and dragged heavy cannon up steep hills. Nelson was in charge of supervising the movement of the guns.

This time, the weather was hot, and the English and French loyalists were attacked by droves of disease-carrying mosquitoes. Many officers and men died of fever. Nelson, himself usually susceptible to the dangers of such a climate, fared well but was wounded by the fragment of an exploding shell, severely limiting the sight in his right eye. Toward the end of his life, Nelson would confide that he was nearly blind because of the wound.

Finally, out of ammunition, the defenders of Calvi surrendered to their debilitated besiegers: 600 French troops lay down their arms before a conquering force of fewer than 400 able-bodied men. Once again, Nelson might have expected commendation for his service, and, once more, he was slighted. In the official report of the action submitted by Lieutenant General the Honourable Charles Stuart, with whom he had worked closely, Captain Nelson's name was omitted completely.

Lord Hood was replaced as Commander in Chief of the Mediterranean by Vice Admiral William Hotham. If Nelson had been hoping for inspirational leadership from his new commander, he was soon disappointed. Intercepting the French fleet on its way to Corsica, Nelson saw a chance to attack two French ships that had collided in their effort to escape the approaching British fleet. The *Agamemnon* loosed broadside after broadside into the larger *Ça Ira*, reducing her to a "perfect wreck," as Captain Nelson described her. Admiral Hotham, however, signaled Nelson to break off his attack and rejoin the line of battle, as the French force had now returned to fight.

The next day, the crippled *Ça Ira* was attacked again and was surrendered to one of Nelson's lieutenants. Nelson urged Admiral Hotham to press the attack against the French, but the latter, knowing his ships to be undermanned, refused.

The *Agamemnon* later encountered the French fleet again. Nelson quickly heeled about to inform Admiral Hotham and the rest of the fleet that lay at anchor at Corsica. Under the threat of the advancing British fleet, the French retreated in the direction of home ports. Light winds spread the fleets over several miles of sea, with Nelson itching to continue the fight. Hotham, however, decided that they had approached too close to the French coast and signaled for the British ships to return to safer waters.

Hotham was soon replaced by Admiral Sir John Jervis, and he and Nelson quickly gained respect for one another. It was under Admiral Jervis that Nelson was to enjoy undeniable success and his first taste of widespread fame and glory.

Jervis promoted Nelson to the rank of commodore, with the latter flourishing under long–deserved recognition. *H.M.S. Agamemnon* captured a convoy of five French ships before her captain took command of the seventy-four-gun *Captain*. The war was not going well for the British, however, and the Admiralty ordered that the Mediterranean be abandoned.

Commodore Nelson bitterly regretted the decision and believed the British fleet was capable of much more than it had shown to date. Nelson once more transferred his pennant, this time to the captured vessel *La Minerve*, to effect the evacuation of Elba.

Leaving Elba, Nelson soon found himself sailing in the midst of the Spanish fleet on a foggy night. Realizing the opportunity within his grasp, the commodore steered *La Minerve* through the Spanish lines before her identity could be determined and made haste to intercept Admiral Jervis and the British fleet.

La Minerve reached the fleet off the Cape of St. Vincent on the morning of February 13, 1797. Jervis agreed with Nelson's assessment and immediately issued orders to attack the Spanish fleet. Nelson was returned to the warship *Captain* for the attack.

The fleets converged at dawn on St. Valentine's Day, with Admiral Sir John ordering his warships to form a single column and sail between the two formations of Spanish ships. Thus the Spanish fleet was cut in two. As Admiral Jervis signaled for his ships to put about one by one, a time-consuming process, Nelson left the line of battle to engage the enemy.

By doing so, the commodore ran the risk of angering his superior officer. He also ran the risk of crushing defeat, but he saw his actions as the only way to give Admiral Jervis's battle plan a chance to work.

The *Captain* exchanged broadsides with no fewer than five Spanish ships of the line. *H.M.S. Excellent*, *Culloden*, and *Blenheim* joined their sister ship, with *Culloden* and *Blenheim* quickly driven back.

With her spars and rigging shot away, the *Captain* was practically incapable of maneuvering. Accordingly, Nelson ordered the ship to ram the eighty-gun *San Nicolas*, which had by now collided with the 112-gun *San Josef*, both of which were larger than Nelson's flagship.

Drawing his sword, Nelson ordered the Spanish ships boarded, and he scrambled after a soldier of the 69th Regiment along the

After a long and frustrating period of inactivity, Commodore Horatio Nelson achieved fame when he led a boarding party against two larger warships.

bowsprit, becoming only the second attacker to board the *San Nicolas*.

The first ship was quickly taken but now a volley of musket fire rained down on the British from the larger *San Josef*. Nelson ordered the sailors and troops aboard the *San Nicolas* reinforced and led the attack on the *San Josef*.

As the commodore swung into the main chains of the warship, a Spanish officer approached and surrendered. The captain of the *San Josef* quickly followed suit, with the officers all surrendering their swords to the victorious Nelson.

The Spanish fleet was routed, and Nelson and Admiral Jervis became the heroes of the day. To England, long accustomed to a diet of nothing but bad news from the war, the victory at sea proved extremely important in terms of morale.

Admiral Sir John Jervis was created Earl St. Vincent for his role in the battle, with Nelson becoming a Knight of the Bath. Shortly thereafter, the country parson's son, now the toast of the nation, found himself promoted to rear admiral.

At thirty-eight, Admiral Sir Horatio Nelson basked in his long-awaited fame. A few months later he would suffer a disastrous defeat at Tenerife, an ill-advised attack that would cost him his right arm but little, if any, of his glory.

He would go on to destroy the French fleet at Aboukir for which he would be made a baron, would earn more glory at Copenhagen, be elevated to viscount, and eventually destroy the combined French and Spanish fleets at Trafalgar, the decisive battle which would cost him his life at the age of forty-seven.

Nelson had gone from being an unemployed captain to one of the most celebrated men in Europe in four short years. And, as often as he had imagined settling down with his wife in some "neat cottage" somewhere, he had embarked at last upon a swift-moving career that would immortalize him as his country's most beloved naval hero.

Across the
Atlantic
in a
Flying Boat

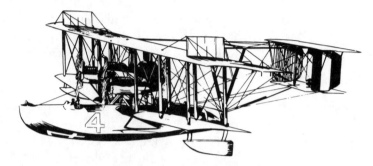

*The NC-4 was the first plane
to cross the Atlantic.*

THE OUTBREAK OF World War I both hurt and helped the cause of transatlantic flight. It hurt in the short term because the war interrupted a contest sponsored by London's *Daily Mail* offering $50,000 to the first team to cross the Atlantic by air. The U.S. Navy had been working closely with Glenn Curtiss—the first man to fly an airplane from the water—in the development of a long-range flying boat. By the end of July 1914, the prototype airplane, the *America*, had finished her trials. The attempt to cross the Atlantic was to be made on August 15, but on August 3, Germany declared war on France and the contest was postponed.

The war raging in Europe and on the high seas soon underscored the need for transatlantic flight. Ships carrying bombers that were to be used in antisubmarine warfare were being sunk by German U-boats. How could the planes do their duty if they never arrived?

The Navy set out to create a plane capable of crossing the Atlantic under its own power, independent of crowded troop and transport ships. Within three days of being summoned by the top brass in the Navy's Construction Corps, Curtiss and his engineers had put together plans for two different "flying boats," both radically different from anything that had been seen before.

Commander G. C. Westervelt named the proposed plane "Navy-Curtiss Number One," which soon gave way to "NC-1." From the start, the project was a joint effort by Navy engineers and their counterparts at Curtiss Aeroplane and Motor Corporation. A free exchange of ideas from both sides left no room for oversize egos—the NC-1 was simply too important. By December 1917, Secretary of the Navy Josephus Daniels was impressed enough by the work to order the construction of four NC-class flying boats.

In July of the following year, aviation experts from England examined the NC aircraft for the second time, and once again went away unimpressed. The British Aviation Commission's official report on the flying boat stated, "The machine is impossible and is not likely to be of any use whatever."

The first test flight of the NC was scheduled for October 4, 1918. Test pilot Commander Holden C. Richardson and a crew of four climbed aboard the seaplane. As a crowd of several hundred looked on, Richardson taxied the NC-1, by now known simply as the *Nancy*, through the water and into the wind. When the wings caught the wind, the largest flying boat in the world roared out of the water and into the bright autumn sky.

When the Armistice was signed a few weeks later, the need for long-range antisubmarine seaplanes was diminished for the time being, but by then the Navy was dedicated to transatlantic flight. Naval aviator Commander John Henry Towers was assigned as officer in charge of the project. Other nations and private firms in the U.S. were already busily working on flying boats of their own in order to win the $50,000 prize that was once again being offered by the *Daily Mail*. The Navy planes would not be eligible for the prize as "ocean stoppages" had been ruled out. Nonetheless, the Navy was determined to complete the first flight, for the glory of America and the service.

Test flights of NC-1 pointed out several flaws in the design of the craft, and the engineers set out to correct these before beginning on NC-2. In the meantime, Commander Westervelt went to work to determine the best route and the best time of year to attempt the crossing. He proposed that ships be stationed at 100-mile intervals along the flight path to serve as navigational aids, weather stations, and rescue vessels in case of emergency.

A fourth engine was added to the NC planes, and the placement of the cockpit was changed. The tentative date for crossing was set as May 5, 1919. Logistics were becoming a headache, since the Navy was now calling for a ship every fifty miles along the route—some eighty vessels in all. Navy and Curtiss personnel worked around the clock until everything was ready on the night of May 4. Early the next morning, fire broke out in the hangar, destroying part of NC-4's tail and one of NC-1's wings.

The men worked heroically to restore the planes, cannibalizing parts from NC-2. By midnight, the planes were ready for flight. But the weather now refused to cooperate, and the flight was indefinitely postponed.

Then the weather suddenly cleared, and on May 8, 1919, NC-1, NC-3, and NC-4, commanded by Lieutenant Commander Patrick Bellinger, Commander John Towers, and Lieutenant Commander Albert Read, respectively, took off from Rockaway Beach, Long Island, on what would become their historic flight.

As the planes headed for Halifax, NC-4 began falling behind— the crew had lost oil pressure in one of the engines and had to shut it down. At 2:05 that afternoon, the same plane lost a connecting rod in a second engine and had to make an emergency landing at sea. The other two flying boats continued their flight, both arriving at Halifax within ten minutes of each other. NC-4, unable to contact a ship by radio, taxied eighty miles to Chatham, Massachusetts.

The next day, NC-1 and NC-3 flew on to Newfoundland, their jumping off point for the transatlantic flight. Weather conditions were unfavorable, so the crews holed up at Trepassey Bay while the press converged on the desolate area. At the same time, engineers worked feverishly to repair the crippled NC-4. On May 15, NC-4 was ready to fly again, and the plane took to the skies to rejoin the other aircraft.

The flight was rough for NC-4, and she was refitted with a new

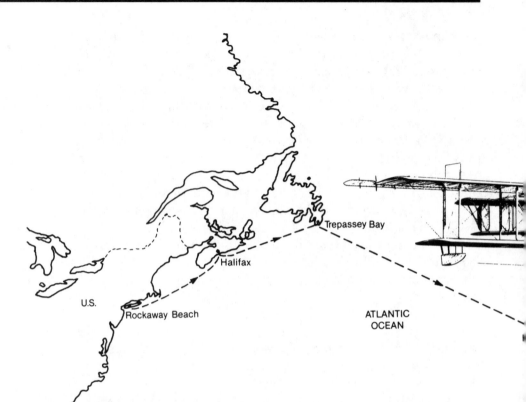

The route of the crossing.

engine and three new propellers. At 5:36 P.M., May 16, the three flying boats left behind the choppy waters of Trepassey and took to the skies.

As the planes flew through the dark night, they soon became separated and lost visual contact with each other. At one point the three were in danger of colliding before the crews spotted one another. Dawn did not help visibility; a heavy fog had rolled in, and rain pelted the fliers.

Just before 9:30 on the morning of May 17, the crew of NC-4 spotted land beneath them—they had reached the Azores, twelve hundred nautical miles from Newfoundland, in fifteen hours and eighteen minutes. After circling, the plane put down at Horta, where the *U.S.S. Columbia* awaited them.

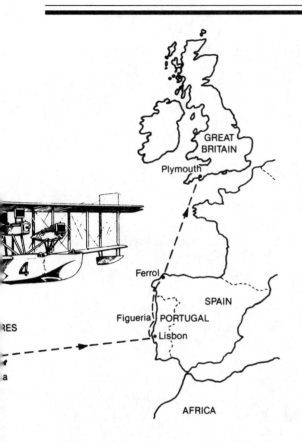

Meanwhile, the crews of the other two aircraft were having difficulties. NC-3 had strayed off course and found herself with only a couple of hours' fuel. Aviator Towers, plane commander, ordered a landing. The seas were rough, and the flying boat was severely damaged when she smacked down on the water. Further flight was impossible; the former flying boat was reduced to merely a boat with wings as she taxied toward the Azores. The crippled plane limped into port two days later.

NC-1 also landed in the twelve-foot seas shortly after eight A.M. on the seventeenth, some hundred miles northwest of the Azores. The crew valiantly attempted to motor to their destination by water before being picked up by the Greek Ship *Ionia*. The plane had sustained severe damage in the rough landing and sank before the Greeks could take her in tow.

In an effort to beat the Americans in the transatlantic race, a British team took off from St. John's, Newfoundland, in a modified Sopwith. The plan called for two aviators, Harry Hawker and Royal Navy Lieutenant Commander McKenzie Grieve, to fly nonstop to Ireland. The two disappeared at sea, however, and the *Daily Mail* announced that it would donate the $50,000 prize to the two men's widows as consolation.

Commander Read and his crew left Ponta Delgada on the morning of May 20, arriving in Lisbon harbor at twilight on May 27, 1919. NC-4 had successfully crossed the Atlantic under her own power, a first in aviation history. On the 30th, the plane took off again, setting down briefly in Ferrol, Spain, before continuing the flight to Plymouth, England.

The grueling trip was over, and many honors were heaped upon the Navy and Coast Guard fliers who had undertaken the dangerous mission. The crew was even more pleased to learn that their British colleagues, Hawker and Grieve, who were believed to have perished at sea, had actually been rescued by a passing ship.

The hoopla soon subsided as others made the flight. British fliers completed the crossing about two weeks later in a Vickers Vimy, and a blimp soon made a round-trip flight between Scotland and New York. Nonetheless, the men of NC-4 had the satisfaction of knowing that they were the first. No matter how many crossings came later, Lieutenant Commander Albert Cushing Read, plane commander; Lieutenant Elmer Stone, U.S. Coast Guard, and Lieutenant (j.g.) Walter Hinton, pilots; Lieutenant James Breese, engineer; Ensign Herbert Rodd, radioman; and Chief Machinist's Mate Eugene Rhoads could always say that they had done what no other men had ever done before.

The NC-4 is currently on display at the National Museum of Naval Aviation in Pensacola, Florida.

Navarino– End of an Era

M EN HAD BEEN GOING to war under sail for centuries. Such classic battles as Lepanto, the defeat of the Spanish Armada and Nelson's bittersweet victory at Trafalgar all come to mind as examples of strategic duels at sea, played out under clouds of canvas, but this era came to a close after the little-known Battle of Navarino Bay in 1827.

The age of sail power was already being threatened. As early as 1824, a steamer had participated in naval warfare in action in Burma, and the Greek War of Independence had also witnessed forays by steamships. Lord Cochrane, the British First Admiral of Greece, had ordered six steamships for the Greek fleet.

The war began in 1821 and quickly won the hearts of such Romantic poets as Wordsworth and Lord Byron. Byron, in fact, died in 1824, in Missolonghi where he had traveled to assist the movement for Greek liberation.

In the 1827 Treaty of London, Great Britain, France, and Russia agreed to secure independence for Greece. All three nations already had officers and men fighting alongside the Greeks. In August, just one month after the treaty was signed, British Admiral Sir Edward Codrington, commander-in-chief of the Mediterranean, met with his French counterpart, Le Comte de Rigny, at Smyrna to discuss impending actions against the Turks. Both admirals were notified that they would receive reinforcements and that a Russian squadron, under the command of Rear Admiral Count Heiden, had sailed to join them. In the meantime, a fleet of Turkish and Egyptian ships sailed for Navarino, where they arrived in the first week of September.

That same week brought news to the British and French fleets that the terms of the armistice had been rejected by the Turks. Admiral Codrington had received orders to "enforce the maintenance of an armistice by sea" and relayed the message to his captains that they were to intercept any shipment of men or arms to the Turks or Egyptians. Such actions were to be carried out peacefully if possible, with force if necessary. Admiral Lord Cochrane's plan to attack the fleets at Navarino was expressly forbidden by Codrington. The fate of the Greeks lay in the hands of the international alliance.

Ibrahim Pasha, Turkish commander-in-chief, ignored the warnings and set sail for Hydra with a sizable fleet. Codrington's five ships were too far north to intercept the Turks, but French Admiral de Rigny appeared with six French vessels and three British ships of the line. The Turks backed down.

The warring factions held a conference three days later, September 25, which erupted in disagreement. The Allies stationed two frigates off Navarino while Ibrahim was to await further instructions from his government. Once the French and British had left, however, the wily Turk weighed anchor. The frigates on picket duty signaled Codrington, who brought the British ships back to Navarino in time to see Ibrahim sailing away.

On October 13, the Russian squadron joined the British, and they sailed toward Ibrahim's fleet, which by then had returned to Navarino. The French caught up with the Allies four days later, and Codrington sent *H.M.S. Dartmouth*, with forty-two guns, into port to protest the continued fighting in the Morea.

Told that Ibrahim was not in port and his whereabouts unknown, the Allied admirals decided to take matters into their own hands and sail en masse into Navarino Bay. Their numbers consisted of twelve

Ibrahim Pasha commanded the Turkish fleet in the last battle fought wholly under sail.

The Allied fleet routed the Turks, assuring independence for Greece.

British, seven French, and eight Russian ships. The Turkish fleet boasted three ships of the line, fifteen frigates, fourteen corvettes, and five brigs. The Egyptian fleet had four frigates, three corvettes, four brigs, and various other smaller vessels.

The Allies set the day for the battle: October 20. The fleet of twenty-seven ships sailed in from the southwest in two lines, the British and French to starboard, the Russians to port. As the warships approached, the Turks sent out a messenger refusing them entrance. Codrington replied that he had come to give orders, not to take them.

The ships sailed into the bay. The crew of a Turkish fire ship fired upon one of the *Dartmouth*'s boats, killing and wounding some of the crew. The British ship dispatched a second boat to help tow the menacing fire ship out of the way, and the boat's officer was killed by musket fire.

Crewmen aboard the *Dartmouth* returned small arms fire, as did men aboard the French ship *Sirene*. A Turkish corvette fired a broadside at the *Sirene*, which returned the volley. At this point, the Battle of Navarino began in earnest.

The fighting was intense as the Allies exchanged cannon fire with the larger Turkish and Egyptian fleet, but the British, French, and Russian ships slowly began gaining the upper hand. One by one, the enemy ships fell silent. The fleet saw fourteen of their largest vessels sunk or destroyed, with only one frigate and fifteen smaller ships surviving serious damage. Casualties for the Turks and Egyptians were estimated at between three and four thousand.

The Allies reported 182 killed and 489 wounded—it was a resounding victory in the fight for Greek independence.

The Battle of Navarino did not end the war, but it effectively ended the war at sea. The fighting dragged on another two years and officially ended in 1829 with the signing of a treaty bestowing independence upon Greece.

Navarino may be largely forgotten by students of history today, but it claims the distinction of being the last sea battle fought wholly under sail, ending a very long chapter in the history of naval warfare.

A
Matter
of
Endurance

The Endurance, *trapped in the ice*.

O CCASIONALLY, men who set out to accomplish a difficult task find that they must do something even more demanding. Such was the situation that Sir Ernest Henry Shackleton faced in his third expedition to the Antarctic.

Shackleton, along with twenty-six other members of the party, had sailed to the southern continent aboard the 144-foot *Endurance* with the goal of becoming the first men to cross the Antarctic overland from west to east. The plan called for landing a ship in the Weddell Sea and traveling by foot and dogsled to the South Pole before continuing on to the Ross Sea. Another party was to cache food between the pole and the Ross Sea for Shackleton's men to use.

This was Shackleton's third expedition to the Antarctic. He had been on Scott's trip in 1901 and had pressed to within 745 miles of the pole. Six years later, Shackleton and three fellow explorers came as close as ninety-seven miles to the pole before being forced to turn back when food supplies ran low.

Now, in 1914, the forty-year-old adventurer sensed the last chance for an old-school epic undertaking. The South Pole had been conquered by the Norwegian explorer Amundsen in 1912, and

Shackleton was feeling that the days of the Polar heroes were rapidly passing.

Funds were raised, a ship purchased, a crew selected, and the journey began. The *Endurance* raised South Georgia Island on November 15, 1914. There the crew received unfavorable reports of ice conditions in the Weddell Sea. Shackleton decided to push on after a month's stay at South Georgia. By January 24, 1915, the *Endurance* lay helplessly trapped in the ice floes. The crew waited nine months while the pressure increased on their ship. They were unable to contact the outside world with their wireless radio, and there were no other means of communication.

On October 27, 1915, Shackleton gave the order to abandon ship. The party was in dire straits, and Shackleton felt his first duty was to his men. He decided to abandon the crossing in favor of trying to get everyone out alive. The band of explorers would walk to the open ocean, he announced, some 300 miles to the northeast. By necessity, they would drag their three boats with them.

Soon after they left her, the *Endurance* was literally crushed to pieces and sank. Two days later, the party began the push toward water. Hauling the boats slowed the progress considerably, as they had to be pulled by teams of men in harnesses. By the end of the first day, the men had covered barely a mile. Shackleton decided to set camp and hope the ice would drift toward their destination. The crew remained at their "Ocean Camp" for two months, existing as best they could, crowded together miserably in their tents, becoming accustomed to the cold and wet. Shackleton, fearing low morale, announced that the march to the sea would resume.

The men traveled for five days, during which they only progressed nine miles. Shackleton advised his men to pitch camp once more, this one being called "Patience Camp." Since they had left behind much of their food supplies at Ocean Camp, each man was rationed one warm drink per day—a mug of hot powdered milk.

The crew of the *Endurance* was destined to spend three and a half months camped precariously on the thinning ice. They survived by killing penguins and an occasional seal for meat. They could do little else but wait.

Sir Ernest Shackleton successfully led his men to safety after facing certain death in the Antarctic.

Late in January 1916, a violent gale-force wind began blowing from the south, driving the ice eighty-four miles in six days. It was enough to renew hope. Early in March, the men felt the unmistakable roll of the sea beneath their feet. Later that month, Shackleton sighted land ahead. The men were helpless in attempts to reach the land, and their floe drifted to the tip of Palmer Peninsula. The only land between their position and the storm-ravaged open sea were the two tiny islands of Clarence and Elephant, about 120 miles to the north.

Almost daily, the ice floe decreased in size. On April 8, the floe split in half, the men on one half, the boats and provisions on the other. The men struggled to rejoin their goods. Just after striking the tents a little while later, the floe was wrenched apart again. It now measured barely fifty yards across.

Shackleton announced his decision: "Launch the boats."

The three boats went into the water, and oarsmen began pulling away from the dangerous floe. They rowed until evening descended. Shackleton picked out a new floe upon which to camp. It looked sturdy enough.

The men pitched their tents and turned in after a cold supper. A few hours later, they were awakened by the sound of splitting ice. The floe cracked directly beneath one of the tents, spilling the eight occupants into the icy water. Seven of them swam out, and Shackleton himself pulled out the eighth man, who had been trapped in his sleeping bag.

At eight the next morning, the adventurers took to their boats again and, after navigating their way through some thick ice, finally found themselves in open sea. It turned out to be a mixed blessing. The boats were pounded by thirty-foot waves, and by two that afternoon the men were exhausted. They pitched camp on an ice floe.

The next morning they set out again and remained in the boats for four days. On the fifth day, the peaks of Elephant Island were sighted, only thirty miles away. The men rowed with renewed determination but found themselves caught in a strong offshore current, complicated by renewed gale winds. Somehow, incredibly, they reached Elephant Island the next day. It was the first time their feet had touched land in well over a year.

The men established a camp in the most sheltered place they could find. Much to their joy, there were plenty of seals and penguins on the island for food, but Shackleton knew that the ordeal was not over. Someone still had to go for a rescue party. The swashbuckling leader announced that he and a crew of five would sail for South Georgia, some 800 miles away.

The ship's carpenter went to work readying the twenty-two-foot *Caird* for the trip. Hundreds of pounds of rocks were placed in the whaleboat as ballast, and a canvas deck was stretched across her. She was supplied with two casks of drinking water and a month's supply of food. On April 24, the *Caird* set sail.

The crew of the tiny whaler experienced the furies of the South Atlantic, skirting gale-force winds and dashing through fifty-foot seas. Nine days after leaving Elephant Island, navigator Worsley, captain of the *Endurance*, plotted their position and announced that they had traveled about 403 miles, about halfway to South Georgia. The gods of nature then saw fit to smile upon the sailors, and for two days the seafarers enjoyed sunny skies and calm winds. The respite did not last, however, and the *Caird* was once more subjected to the punishing storms of the South Atlantic.

Worsley's calculations had to be as accurate as possible for the crew to reach the island, which was only twenty-five miles wide. Beyond the island was nothing but three thousand miles of open water.

By May 7, the crew was worried. According to Worsley's plottings, the boat should have been only a few miles offshore, but no land was visible. It was not until mid-morning of the next day that they sighted land, just ten miles ahead. As they drew closer, the men saw the rough surf pounding mercilessly on the shore of the island; it was impossible to land. Shackleton had the boat go about and head out to sea. A violent storm came up, and the *Caird* rode it out over the next thirty-six hours.

They finally reached shore on the afternoon of May 10, 1916. As joyous as that was, the men were on the wrong side of the island. In order to reach any of the four whaling stations on South Georgia, they would have to cross over the jagged mountains and treacherous glaciers. Shackleton decided to rest his men for eight days before pushing on.

On May 19, Shackleton, Worsley, and second officer Tom Crean set off for civilization. For seven exhausting hours, the three men climbed up the first of the four mountains they had to conquer. Upon reaching the summit, they discovered that the other side offered a sheer drop. Shackleton and his two officers searched frantically for a safe way to descend. Finally, Shackleton suggested that they slide down the 1,500–foot drop.

The men sat down, toboggan style, using coils of rope as cushions, and slid down the slope as one. Two minutes later, they safely reached the bottom and piled into a snowbank from which they all emerged laughing. Night was setting in, and they had traveled only nine of the twenty-nine miles they had to cover. They struggled on, climbing more ranges and even dropping through an icy waterfall. At four the next afternoon, they reached the whaling station at Stromness.

That night, Worsley set out aboard a whaling ship and rescued the three men left on the other side of the island. Two days later, Shackleton mounted a rescue operation to retrieve the twenty-two castaways on Elephant Island. Weather hampered this and two subsequent attempts, and it was not until the afternoon of August 30 that the remaining crew members of the ill-fated *Endurance* were rescued.

Despite the hardships the men had endured during their long struggle for survival, not one man had been lost from the original party. The adventure was far greater than any of them could have expected when they sailed from England two years earlier.

Revenue Cutters and the Battle of New Orleans

A S DEVELOPMENTS UNFOLDED elsewhere in the War of 1812, forces began gathering for the final engagement—the Battle of New Orleans. The British fleet loitered off Pensacola, and Major General Andrew Jackson had established his headquarters at Mobile, anxiously awaiting the arrival of militia troops from Tennessee, Mississippi, and Kentucky.

Jackson reasoned that, given the nature of the water routes to New Orleans—the well-defended Mississippi River and the tricky, shallow lakes and bayous, the British would attack overland and probably would march through Mobile. Accordingly, he dispatched Major William Lawrence of the Second Infantry and 130 soldiers to Fort Bowyer (the site of latter-day Fort Morgan) at the mouth of Mobile Bay.

Old Hickory had received an intelligence report in the form of two letters written by Vincent Gray, an American citizen in Havana, which outlined a planned attack on Fort Bowyer, the British landing at Pensacola, and an invasion of New Orleans. One of the letters had been forwarded by the pirate Jean Lafitte, and both had passed through the hands of Louisiana Governor William C. C. Claiborne before finding their way to Jackson.

The Americans occupying Fort Bowyer did not have to wait long. On September 15, 1814, the British attacked the fort by land and sea. Several hundred Creek and Choctaw Indians, dressed in British redcoats and shepherded by Royal Marines, attacked along the sandy peninsula leading to Fort Bowyer.

Captain Sir William H. Percy's four warships, armed with ninety guns and a combined complement of more than 600 sailors and Marines, began a bombardment of the fort.

From inside the fort, Major Lawrence returned fire in both directions. Percy's flagship, *H.M.S. Hermes*, was disabled under the withering fire and ran aground. Her crew set the frigate ablaze and transferred to *H.M.S. Sophie*. The Marines and Indians fared no better, soon finding themselves pinned down under the fort's barrage.

The battle ended with the land troops retreating to Pensacola. Captain Percy's Gulf squadron retired to the waters off Apalachicola. British casualties included 162 dead and seventy-two wounded. The Americans suffered four men killed and five wounded.

General Jackson then accused the Spanish Governor of West Florida, Gonzalez Manrique, of aiding and abetting belligerent British troops and inciting the Indians to attack American interests. Despite protests of innocence on the part of the Spaniard, Jackson and an army of 3,000 marched on Pensacola, taking the city with relative ease. The British retreated from Fort Barrancas and put to sea.

An overland attack thus prevented, twenty-nine-year-old U.S. Navy Commodore Daniel Todd Patterson began piecing together his forces at New Orleans. His fleet consisted of six sloops armed with five guns each, the fourteen-gun U.S. Revenue *Marine*, Cutter *Carolina*, the *Louisiana* (which may or may not have been a revenue cutter) and the Lighthouse Service Cutters *Seahorse* and *Alligator*.

Patterson left the crewless *Louisiana* riding at a levee and deployed his sloops on Lake Borgne, to the east of New Orleans, and along the Mississippi Sound in the event the British attacked from that direction. At Jamaica, learning of the defeats at Mobile and

Pensacola, the British decided that the route of attack would be through Lake Borgne.

Whatever happened on other fields of battle—no matter what was decided by the peace commissioners at Ghent, Belgium—it was imperative that the British take and control New Orleans. Once the vital seaport was securely in British hands 10,000 troops poised in Canada could sweep down the Mississippi River, cutting off further westward American expansion.

Andrew Jackson was just as determined to prevent the Crescent City from falling to the British. Depositing troops in Pensacola and Mobile, he left the latter on November 21, headed for New Orleans on horseback.

The British fleet sailed from Jamaica four days later, under the command of Vice Admiral Sir Alexander Forrester Inglis Cochrane and a youthful Major General John Keane. Their forces consisted of 8,000 troops, 10,000 sailors, 1,500 Marines, and another 500 engineers and artillerymen.

In all, some fifty vessels sailed from Negril Bay, including numerous merchant ships confidently chartered to haul prizes that no doubt would be taken at New Orleans. Aboard his flagship *Tonnant*, Admiral Cochrane expected an easy victory, despite the knowledge that his plans were known by the Americans.

Jackson arrived in New Orleans on December 1, after inspecting possible routes of attack and their defenses. The British could follow at least seven routes. Excluding sailing up the Mississippi River, the remaining routes relied on passage through shallow and tortuous bayous, most of which could be defended fairly well.

Jackson's appearance in New Orleans was less than inspiring. Soaking wet and wearing nearly threadbare clothes, the general was suffering from dysentery and looked gaunt. When he addressed the citizens through an interpreter, however, he came alive, promising to drive their enemies "into the sea, or perish in the effort." From the crowd arose the cry, "Vive Jackson!"

Next came the process of putting together a respectable defense force, made up of regular Army troops, militia men, local dragoons, and a hodgepodge of citizen soldiers, including "free men of color."

Major General Andrew Jackson organized a hodge-podge army to fight the British at New Orleans.

Jackson's unlikely ally in the fight was the dashing pirate, Jean Lafitte.

Arms and men were en route from elsewhere and more arrived daily, but Jackson's "army" was small and underarmed.

Commodore Patterson loaned additional firepower to Jackson's forces in the form of muskets and artillery pieces from the Navy Depot at New Orleans. Patterson also dispatched the cutters *Seahorse* and *Alligator* to join the gunboats patrolling Lake Borgne and the Mississippi Sound.

Since British Admiral Cochrane had not received the shallow draft vessels he had requested, he abandoned his original plan of attacking New Orleans by way of Lake Pontchartrain and decided to land at Bayou Bienvenu. *H.M.S. Sophie*, commanded by Captain Lockyer, was sent ahead to engage and destroy the waiting American gunboats.

Commanding the American fleet was U.S. Navy Lieutenant

Thomas Catesby Jones who sighted the British ships on December 12. Two gunboats fired upon Lockyer's vessels before retreating into Lake Borgne. The next day, on board the British transport *Fox*, Lieutenant George Cleig wrote: "Five large cutters, armed with six heavy guns each, were seen at anchor in the distance, and . . . all endeavors to land, till these were captured, would have been useless. . . ."

The British offloaded barges that had been built in Jamaica and attacked the cutter *Seahorse*, which had been detached to guard a small American battery and arsenal at Bay St. Louis. The little tender valiantly battled with seven barges for half an hour before Sailing Master Johnson ordered the arsenal, battery, and cutter destroyed to prevent their falling into enemy hands.

Lieutenant Jones and his gunboats retreated before the advancing British force of forty-five barges. On the morning of December 14, having lost the wind and tide and being cut off from further retreat, Jones arranged his five gunboats in a line of battle to the northwest of Malheureux Island, at the mouth of Lake Borgne.

As the barges approached, the cutter *Alligator*, which earlier had been sent back to New Orleans to inform Commodore Patterson of events, appeared on the horizon. Four British barges intercepted and captured the cutter.

Outmanned seven to one and shipping only half as many guns, the American fleet nevertheless managed to sink several of the barges, killing seventeen and wounding seventy-seven. Jones, himself wounded, lost fifteen killed and thirty-five wounded. The battle was over by one in the afternoon, with the Americans taken prisoner and their ships manned by British prize crews.

Despite its defeat in this "Battle of the Barges" it has been argued that the American squadron delayed the British advance by six to nine days. The battle bought Andrew Jackson valuable time in which to strengthen his defenses of New Orleans.

The Louisiana legislature authorized funding to man the crewless *Louisiana*, offering twenty-four dollars to volunteers for three month's enlistment. General Jackson thought the measure too weak and, on December 16, placed New Orleans under martial law.

A Creole leader, Bernard de Marigny, approached Jackson with the idea of enlisting Jean Lafitte and his Baratarians in the fight against the British. Lafitte's attorney, Edward Livingston, also tried to persuade Jackson.

The British had unsuccessfully attempted to recruit Lafitte and his men, offering the swashbuckler a commission as captain in the Royal Navy and a bonus of $30,000. Lafitte's refusal may have had more to do with greed than any sense of patriotism. By swearing allegiance to the British, Lafitte would also be agreeing to give up his pursuit of prizes on the high seas.

General Jackson, who had once described Lafitte and his followers as "hellish banditti," had no desire to employ men whom he considered common criminals. Despite his popularity and his insistence that he held legal letters of marque as a privateer, Lafitte knew the government frowned upon his activities. By joining Jackson, he saw a chance for amnesty.

Lafitte himself finally met with General Jackson, offering his services, a thousand men, flints, powder, and shot. He also promised to provide a seasoned crew for the idle *Louisiana*. His well-trained gunners would be indispensable aboard the cutters as well as in the forts and trenches. Jackson soon came to admire Lafitte and counted on him as a trusted ally.

Governor Claiborne issued a proclamation declaring a "Free and Full Pardon" for Lafitte's men who volunteered to serve with Jackson. Lafitte and his followers organized artillery groups, and one of Jackson's scouts, Pierre Jugeat, raised a company of Choctaws to guard the wilderness approaches to the city.

On December 23, after rowing across Lake Borgne for more than five days, the British landed at Bayou Bienvenu and established headquarters at the Villeré plantation. General Jackson sought naval support and marched on the British.

Patterson dispatched the cutter *Carolina*, complete with gun crews trained by Lafitte. On the evening of the twenty-third, the *Carolina* hove to within sight of the enemy's campfires, and Captain John Henley gave the order to fire upon the British. That signaled the American ground forces to attack.

The battle raged in the darkness. Demoralized, the surprised

British managed to rally, but confusion reigned among the ranks. They would later complain bitterly of this "uncivilized warfare."

During the next few days, the *Carolina* and the newly arrived *Louisiana* rained a constant storm of shells on the British, day and night. Lieutenant General Sir Edward Michael Pakenham, the new British commanding officer, arrived to find his troops in disarray. He and Admiral Cochrane agreed that the guns of the *Carolina* and *Louisiana* must be silenced.

A naval cannon was moved into the British camp and a furnace built to make hot shot. On December 27, the British opened fire on the cutter *Carolina*. The second volley lodged in the main hold, and the cutter caught fire. Captain Henley gave the order to abandon ship, managing to salvage a thirty-two-pounder cannon before the cutter exploded and sank. The *Louisiana* escaped to safety.

The *Louisiana* continued to provide covering fire in the following days, and when the final battle began at Chalmette on January 8, 1815, gun crews from the cutter landed and joined Jackson's troops and the gunners from the *Carolina* to defeat the British.

The actions of the U.S. Revenue Marine and U.S. Lighthouse Service cutters and crews added significantly to the American success at New Orleans in a battle which, if lost, could have meant the dissolution of the United States or, at the very least, the end of westward expansion.

The
Cruise of
the
Sea Devil

ON THE MORNING OF January 9, 1917, the British freighter *Gladys Royale*, out of Cardiff and bound for Buenos Aires, sighted an aging Norwegian bark signaling for a chronometer reading. It was a usual enough request for a windjammer, and the steamer slowed and moved to windward to accommodate the merchantman.

To the British crew's surprise, the sailing vessel raised the German ensign and exposed a 10.5-cm gun. The *Gladys Royale* tried to run from the strange warship but stopped after three shots were fired across her bow. The British steamer surrendered to the German raider, becoming the first victim of Count Felix von Luckner, the man who would soon be known as the "Sea Devil."

The likelihood of an armed sailing vessel in the Imperial German Navy in 1917 seemed fantastic. The Great War was truly the first "modern" war. Surface vessels were heavily armored steamships boasting huge guns, and the introduction of the U-boat had set terror in the hearts of ships' captains around the world.

The fact that no one expected a sailing vessel to be a modern warship was one of the reasons von Luckner was confident about his project. German Admiralty had rejected the idea as ludicrous. Von

Luckner suspected, as did the Kaiser, that the British Admiralty would feel the same, and therefore never expect an armed windjammer.

Von Luckner had long been defiant of tradition. Coming from a family of distinguished cavalrymen, young Felix heard the call of the sea and ran away from home to serve as a cabin boy. He was only thirteen, and it was the beginning of a romantic adolescence. The youth jumped ship in Australia to woo a restaurant-keeper's daughter and held various odd jobs, everything from selling religious tracts to hunting kangaroos. Von Luckner shipped out again and sailed around the world, partaking in adventures, pulling mischievous pranks, but above all else, learning to sail well and developing a deep respect and love for sailing ships.

When he was twenty, von Luckner returned to Germany to study navigation. After passing the course, he joined the German merchant marine and became a petty officer. The next year, he joined the German Naval Reserve and received his commission.

The young man now felt that he could return home. His family, who had given up all hope of ever seeing him again, joyously received the dashing officer. Von Luckner set about making a name for himself in the Navy. When he was thirty-one, he was admitted to the regular Navy for active duty.

The nobleman won fame when, on different occasions, he rescued five people from drowning. Each time, the officer refused to accept medals for his actions, but he attracted the attention of Kaiser Wilhelm and was given a variety of choice assignments.

When war broke out, von Luckner participated in the battles of Heligoland and Jutland. During the latter clash, the officer was badly wounded and lost his cruiser.

In July 1915, the Scottish-built bark *Pass of Balmaha* was taken as a prize by a British cruiser. The next morning, possession of the windjammer again changed hands when she was captured by the German submarine *U-36*. Taken into port, the *Pass of Balmaha* was rechristened *Seeadler*, and work was begun to refit the ship as a raider.

The vessel was to be disguised as a Norwegian trader. Von Luckner was fluent in Norwegian, and he handpicked a crew of sixty-four men, sixteen of whom were also fluent in the language. The ship was converted into a labyrinth of trick panels and hidden compartments. Quarters to accommodate 400 prisoners were constructed, and the ship was refitted with a second auxiliary diesel engine.

Von Luckner himself traveled to Copenhagen to steal a Norwegian logbook for the *Seeadler*. The German raider, now equipped with two 10.5-cm guns and two machine guns, was to sail under the assumed identity of the *Maleta*, a real Norwegian trader. When sailing orders for the raider were delayed, however, it became necessary to choose a new name—the real *Maleta* had long since sailed.

Finally, von Luckner had the ship smashed up and everything drenched with seawater, including the ship's log. Then the ingenious officer had the ship's carpenter repair everything as it would have been repaired at sea. Thus, the bark, now disguised as the merchantman *Hero*, looked as if she had been damaged in a storm, and her log was conveniently blotted in certain areas.

Just before Christmas 1916, the *Seeadler* set sail as the *Hero*. With the help of gale-force winds, the raider slipped through the Allies' mines, and the ship began her prowl.

On Christmas Day, she was hailed by the British cruiser *Avenger*, which was on blockade duty. The *Seeadler* crew, dressed in wooden shoes and thick sweaters, paid little attention as the boarding officer was welcomed aboard and introduced to the burly von Luckner, who was calling himself Captain Knudson. Knudson made a fierce figure, swearing and spitting tobacco juice as he led the British officer down into his quarters. There, among a mess of scattered papers and underwear, the captain introduced his wife, Josephine (admirably portrayed by a young crewman named Schmidt).

As the boarding officer inspected the ship's logbook, Captain Knudson and his wife made small talk in Norwegian. After some time, the British officer made it clear that he understood the language. Everything was in order, he announced, and the *Hero* was free to continue her course to Australia, pending a signal from the

Count Felix von Luckner waged a most civilized war in a most uncivilized time.

Avenger. The British ship steamed directly toward the *Hero*, swerving at the last possible moment, signaling, "Bon Voyage."

The *Seeadler*, was free—she had been boarded by the enemy and released. The German ensign was hoisted, the crew donned their naval uniforms, and everyone celebrated Christmas with beer and schnapps.

On the morning of January 9, the *Seeadler* took her first prize, the *Gladys Royale*. The freighter's crew was placed in the comfortable prisoners' quarters, and the *Gladys Royale* was sunk.

The next day saw the sailing vessel come across another steamer. Von Luckner signaled his request for a chronometer reading, but the enemy vessel ignored his plea. The German colors were run up and a warning shot was fired. The steamer, a British freighter named the *Lundy Island*, tried to flee. Von Luckner ordered his crew to fire into the steamer's hull and smokestack. The *Lundy Island* surrendered, and her crew was ushered aboard the *Seeadler*.

Von Luckner was very particular as to how his prisoners were to be treated. Their quarters were comfortable and were stocked with games, books, and phonograph records in both French and English. The prisoners were confined to quarters only when the *Seeadler* was going into action. They ate and drank well and were treated as equals by the German sailors. In fact, the prisoners were allowed to compete for the fifty-dollars-and-champagne bonus given to the first man who sighted the next ship.

On January 21, the *Seeadler* sighted the French windjammer, *Charles Gounod*. She was captured and sunk, only after the Germans had relieved the ship of part of her cargo of red wine.

Three days later, the Canadian schooner *Perce* was taken, and on February 3, the German raider spied the French four-masted bark *Antonin*. The *Seeadler* gave chase to the smart French vessel and, out of a sense of sportsmanship—as well as pride—von Luckner refused to engage his diesels.

Only when the two ships had sailed into squall was the German vessel able to overtake her prey. The French captain had taken in his royals and upper topgallant sails in the storm; von Luckner had ignored the winds and continued to sail under full canvas. The Frenchman was seized and sunk.

Before a week was out, the *Seeadler* had added the *Buenos Aires*, an Italian sailing vessel, to a growing list of victims.

All was going well for von Luckner. He had rather easily taken six vessels, two of them steamers. The thing that pleased him most was that there had not been a single casualty. In the midst of one of the most atrocious wars that man has inflicted on man, a war noted for its foul play and extensive and effective use of submarines, machine guns, and chemical warfare, Lieutenant Commander Count Felix von Luckner was, like his predecessor Commander Karl von Müller, waging a most civilized, "old-fashioned" type of war. His would be the last great military command of a sailing vessel.

Indeed, the whole *Seeadler* affair was an anachronism, and in part that lent the success of the operation. Word of a German raider had reached Allied ports, and commercial shipping was in a panic, scared to death of the "Sea Devil" that was plundering ships with apparent ease.

On February 19, 1917, the raider raised the British four-masted bark *Pinmore*. This must have caused von Luckner to have ambivalent feelings. He had served aboard the *Pinmore* in his bohemian days and felt a great love for the ship. Nonetheless, the vessel was captured and her crew taken prisoner. To his crew's surprise, von Luckner rowed over to the *Pinmore* and spent some time wandering around the empty vessel.

Taking a great risk, von Luckner decided to sail the *Pinmore* into Rio de Janeiro to take on fresh supplies. The captured British ship boldly went into Rio. Incredibly, the Germans were able to pull off the caper in much the same way that they had fooled the boarding officer from the *Avenger*.

While in port, von Luckner was told by a British officer that his ship, the *Glasgow*, was to join another British cruiser, the *Amethyst*, in her search for a German raider that had been sighted somewhere west of Trinidad. Von Luckner hurried aboard the *Pinmore*, set sail, and rendezvoused with the *Seeadler* three days later. The *Pinmore* was sent to the bottom, another casualty of war.

The barks *British Yeoman* and *Rochfoucauld* were captured in late February, and on March 5, the French bark *Dupleix* was taken. Her captain felt chagrined, since he had been warned of the German raider's presence. It was with great relief that the Frenchman discovered that the two friends who had warned him were themselves now prisoners aboard the *Seeadler*.

The next week, the raider discovered the large British steamer *Horngarth*. The ship ignored von Luckner's request for a chronometer reading. The Germans then set a phony fire on board the *Seeadler* and signaled for assistance, but the *Horngarth* was not biting. In desperation, von Luckner ordered the young sailor who had portrayed his wife to don his costume and parade about on deck. This got the attention of the British sailors. As the men gathered at the ship's railing to cheer the "woman," von Luckner hoisted the German ensign and began shooting at the steamer's radio shack. A direct hit destroyed the room, thus making it impossible for the *Horngarth* to radio anyone concerning their plight.

The British crew sprang into action. Their steamer was armed with a five-inch gun. The Germans had constructed a fake cannon from an old smokestack, which was now swung into plain view and "fired." Three men, armed only with megaphones and good English, shouted in unison, "Torpedoes clear!" The British ship surrendered.

The *Horngarth* was the biggest prize taken by the *Seeadler*, and she provided the crew and prisoners with plenty of champagne and cognac. The taking of the steamer, though, was the beginning of the end for the German raider. In firing on the radio shack, the Germans had accidentally killed a British officer. Von Luckner regretted this first casualty, and the officer was buried at sea with full military honors. The *Horngarth* was the last ship the Seeadler would sink in the Atlantic.

Ten days after she had taken the *Horngarth*, the *Seeadler* captured the French bark *Cambronne*. Instead of sinking her, von Luckner turned the vessel into a liberty ship. The German raider's holds were bulging with the captured crews of eleven ships. Von Luckner knew that he was taking a chance in turning his prisoners loose, but it was a calculated risk. As captain of the *Cambronne*, the German chose the former captain of the *Pinmore*, making him promise to contact no other ship before reaching Rio. The topmasts of the French ship were cut out to slow her progress. The *Seeadler* sailed north until the *Cambronne* was out of sight. Von Luckner then came about and raced for Cape Horn.

Upon reaching Rio de Janeiro, von Luckner's former captives made their report to the authorities. A small fleet of British cruisers and auxiliaries was raised and dispatched to the Cape Horn area, but the *Seeadler* had effected her escape to the Pacific.

The raider went empty-handed for a couple of months before

capturing and sinking three American four-masted schooners in June and July off the west coast of South America. The *Seeadler* was low on supplies of fresh food, and those age-old ship scourges, beriberi and scurvy, had broken out on board. To remedy this, the raider anchored off the island of Mopelia, in the Society Islands at the end of July. The crew and their prisoners feasted on island delicacies that night. The men were content to rest and regain their health after the rigorous seven-month cruise.

All was well until two days after dropping anchor when the *Seeadler* was wrecked. Von Luckner and his crew were to swear that a tidal wave wrecked their beloved ship, but the American prisoners told a different story. According to the Americans, the raider was anchored too close to the island's jagged reefs. While most of the Germans were ashore, the *Seeadler* drifted onto the reefs and was destroyed.

All too soon, the monotony of island life, as pleasant as it was, began to take its toll on von Luckner. Along with five crewmen, the captain outfitted a lifeboat with a mast, sails, weapons, and food. Von Luckner and his men sailed westward for twenty-eight days before reaching Fiji. Their open boat voyage had covered 2,300 miles. Upon reaching the island, the six men were arrested by the five British soldiers stationed there and were sent to New Zealand for internment until the end of the war.

In all, the *Seeadler* had captured or sunk fifteen ships, three of them steamers, during her 30,000-mile, seven-month cruise. It was estimated that she had intercepted some $25 million in cargo and caused many other vessels to delay their departures. And all of this resulted in only one casualty. It was a record of which any officer would have been proud.

When the war was over, Count Felix von Luckner was released and celebrated as a hero by both sides.

The
Thin Gray
Line

I N THE EARLY DAYS OF World War II, German U-boats were able to destroy merchant ships at will, and Britain's merchant marine, the greatest merchant fleet in the world, soon found itself in real trouble. When merchant ships were organized into convoys, the U-boats simply began hunting in "wolf packs," proving there was no safety in numbers for Allied shipping.

During 1940 and 1941 German submarines sank more than six million tons of shipping belonging to non-Axis nations. When America entered the war, the U.S. merchant marine soon began losing a ship a day. By March 1942, the enemy was sinking two merchant ships on a daily basis. During the war the merchant marine lost more than 5,500 men and nearly a thousand ships, mostly to the wolf packs.

The British Admiralty began a program to build emergency wartime transports, and the first of these, the *Empire Liberty*, was constructed at the Sunderland yard of J. L. Thompson and Sons. It soon became apparent that the British did not have the means to produce the merchant ships in the numbers they needed.

In September 1940, a group of Britons arrived in America, authorized to order the construction of sixty new merchantmen.

The freighters they wanted were uncomplicated, based on the design of the 1879 tramp steamer *Dorington Court*. They would burn coal because oil had become a precious commodity in England, and they would employ a simple reciprocating steam engine instead of steam turbines.

The problem encountered by the British in America was that all the major shipyards in the United States were engaged in building warships. A consortium of smaller yards, led by the New York-based Todd Shipyards joined forces and bid on the project. The newly formed Todd-California Shipbuilding Company proposed to build all sixty freighters in two new yards, one at Richmond, California, on San Francisco Bay, and the other in South Portland, Maine, in conjunction with Bath Iron Works. The British had little choice but to accept. Simultaneously, they signed deals with Canadian firms to build an addition 116 transports.

The man who would prove integral to the building process was Henry J. Kaiser, a construction mogul with absolutely no experience in shipbuilding. He was, however, a man of tremendous energy and foresight. His innovative methods and incentive programs had built the Boulder, Bonneville, and Grand Coulee dams in record time, and his construction projects ranged from subways to roads to the third set of locks on the Panama Canal.

The shipyards Kaiser built were like no other, and he brought mass-production techniques to the science of shipbuilding. Designs were standardized among the Canadian and U.S. plants, and components were assembled all over the country, to be shipped to wherever they were needed first. The engines, for example, were manufactured by seventeen separate builders in the United States and Canada. More shipyards were built as needed, each a little more streamlined than its predecessor.

The first British freighter finished at the Richmond yard, the *Ocean Vanguard*, was completed shortly after America entered the war. All British merchantmen built in the United States would carry the first name *Ocean*, while the ships built for Britain in Canada would bear the prefix *Fort*. Canada built transports for its own use, which began with the name *Park*.

Even before America was pulled into the war by the bombing of Pearl Harbor, it became apparent that the nation needed its own massive shipbuilding program. President Roosevelt announced in February 1941, that America would begin building these "dreadful looking objects" for its own shipping needs. In 1939 and 1940, only 102 ocean-going vessels had been constructed in the United States, but the U.S. Maritime Commission would go on to build no fewer than 2,710 of these steamers, officially designated as EC-2 ships.

Admiral Emory Scott Land, chairman of the U.S. Maritime Commission, dubbed the U.S. fleet of merchant ships the "Liberty Fleet," inspired by the names of such British vessels as the *Empire Liberty* and the *Ocean Liberty*, the second British ship completed in the U.S. In addition to the *Ocean-* and *Fort-*class steamers it purchased, Britain would subsequently receive 200 Liberty ships during the war.

The first Liberty ship, the *Patrick Henry*, was launched at the Bethlehem-Fairfield shipyard in Baltimore on September 27, 1941. It was the beginning of a shipbuilding program the likes of which the world had never seen before or since.

The Liberties basically followed the design of the *Ocean*-class ships built for the British, with some minor alterations. The American version burned oil as fuel instead of coal. The introduction of fewer double-carved plates meant less skilled labor was needed. Other modifications included a new rudder design and the regrouping of all crew quarters in the deck and bridge structure, slightly aft of amidships.

The Liberty ships measured 441 feet 6 inches in length, with a beam of just under fifty-seven feet. They displaced 14,257 tons and had a draft of approximately twenty-eight feet. The Liberties could carry slightly more tonnage than their British-bound counterparts—a total of 9,146 tons of cargo. The ships were not pretty, nor were they particularly fast. Top-rated speed of the Liberties was eleven knots.

Modified Liberty ships included sixty-three tankers, twenty-four colliers, thirty-six boxed aircraft transports, eight tank carriers, and six hospital ships. The transports could also be altered to carry mules or soldiers, although they apparently proved unpopular with troops because of their tendency to roll somewhat excessively. (The mules were not known to complain.)

Across the nation 1.5 million workers were employed in building the Liberty ships. Components (some 30,000 of them went into each vessel) were purchased from 500 plants in thirty-two states. Assembly-line construction was used to preassemble huge sections of the transports.

The prefabricated parts—the largest of which weighed seventy-two tons—were then set in place by enormous cranes in the shipyards. Even the wiring and pipe connections for steam, water, and fuel were set in place ahead of time. Unlike most earlier ships, the Liberties were arc-welded together, not riveted. This sped up construction even more. Kaiser made the mass production of ships a science—a very efficient and profitable science at that.

The Maritime Commission paid a flat fee for each completed ship, but it also paid bonuses for vessels built in less than the allotted time. Even though eighty percent of Kaiser's workers had no experience as shipfitters, they became so adept at building the Liberty ships that they routinely broke records for completion time. Throughout the war, the expected completion time for a Liberty ship decreased substantially. Nationwide the construction time for one of the ships was cut by eighty percent in only two years.

The fastest a ship could be constructed during World War I was seven months. The construction of Liberties was so streamlined that ships were being turned out in a matter of days. Kaiser's Richmond shipyard set the record for the fastest Liberty ship built during the war. Responding to a record set by the Kaiser yard in Portland, Oregon, in which a Liberty was built in ten days in September 1942, the Richmond yard began assembling Hull 440—the *Robert E. Peary*—that November.

Within two hours of beginning construction, the *Peary*'s bottom shell had been laid on Shipway No. 1. Ten hours later the engine was in place. After two days, the hull had been completed up to the upper deck. The superstructure was set in place the third day, and the fourth day was spent painting and wiring. The ship was ready in four

A typical Liberty ship, the Jeremiah O'Brien *came off the ways in June 1943.*
BELOW: *The O'Brien saw service in the Atlantic, the Mediterranean, and the*
Pacific. Today she is a floating museum in San Francisco. PHOTOS COURTESY
NATIONAL LIBERTY SHIP MEMORIAL.

days, fifteen hours, and thirty minutes. The record-breaking time stands as a testament to wartime achievement.

While the much-needed ships were built with speed—three a day by 1942—they were far from perfect. Given the high attrition rate of merchantmen, the Liberties were designed for no more than about five years of service. Many of those that were not torpedoed or bombed lasted not even that long.

The speed of their construction and the new technology (new, at least, to shipbuilding) of arc welding combined to create a number of structural failures in the Liberties. A few actually broke in half while underway; others merely lost their propellers in mid-ocean.

In cold weather and rough seas the Liberty ships were particularly vulnerable to stress fractures. A crack would appear in the hull, usually starting at the corner of some sharply angled hatch, and race across the ship, through welded joints. To counter the problem, rounded corners were adopted, and rivets reinforced certain vital welded areas. A tougher grade of steel was employed, and fractures dropped by an impressive eighty percent by the end of the war.

The Liberties were merchantmen, not warships, but each carried light armament and a detachment of Navy Armed Guard aboard. Gun platforms were fitted on the bows and sterns of the steamers. Navy Armed Guard contingents ranged from eight to twenty-four men under the command of a sole officer. Their only job was to man the guns in case of attack.

A story that is fairly representative of the Armed Guard is the case of the *Nathaniel Hawthorne*. Making her return from the Persian Gulf in November 1942, the ship was struck by two torpedoes north of Trinidad. The ship went down in less than two minutes, but the Armed Guard officer on board, Lieutenant (j.g.) Kenneth Muir, though badly injured, was able to organize an evacuation of the doomed vessel. Again and again Lieutenant Muir braved the flames to guide merchant sailors to the stern of the sinking ship and help them into the water. The officer went down with the ship, along with the rest of his gunners. He was awarded the Navy Cross posthumously.

Weapons aboard the Liberties consisted of twenty-mm, forty-mm, three-inch .50-calibers, and five-inch .38s. And while there were many instances of heroism—the Liberty ship *Stephen Hopkins* mortally wounded the German cruiser *Stier* before sinking—the Navy Armed Guard obviously was no match for the menacing U-boats. Of the 2,710 Liberty ships built, 943 were sunk by enemy action—no less than thirty-five percent.

Liberty ships were constructed through June 1945. Kaiser built more than any other company, launching nearly 700 of the vessels. In 1943, a bigger, faster merchantman was introduced: the Victory ship. Slightly longer than the Liberties, the Victories were powered by steam turbine instead of a reciprocating engine and boasted a maximum speed of seventeen knots.

After the war a number of Liberty ships were scrapped. Some were sold to England, Italy, Greece, France, Norway, and China, and many were still in operation as late as the 1960s. Others were operated as American-flagged merchantmen, and the rest were mothballed for years as part of the Defense Reserve Fleet.

The Defense Reserve Fleet was eventually disbanded, and today there are only two Liberty ships in operating condition, the *S. S. Jeremiah O'Brien* and the *S.S. John W. Brown*, both of which serve as floating museums, memorials to the men and women who built and served aboard the Liberties.

Named for the hero of America's first naval engagement of the Revolutionary War, the *Jeremiah O'Brien* was built by the New England Shipbuilding Corp. in South Portland, Maine. Her keel was laid May 6, 1943, and the *O'Brien* was launched June 19 of the same year. She was chartered by the War Shipping Administration to the Grace Line and made four voyages between the United States and Britain from July 1943 to October 1944. She completed eleven shuttle runs between England and Normandy and participated in the D-Day invasion before returning to America.

On her fifth passage out of the East Coast, the *Jeremiah O'Brien* steamed through the Panama Canal to Chile and Peru before returning to New Orleans. She operated in the South Pacific from July 1945, until January 1946, earning six decorations for her wartime service, including the Merchant Marine Combat Bar, the Atlantic, Pacific, Mediterranean/Middle East War Zone bars, the Philippine Liberation Medal, and the Victory Medal.

After the war the *Jeremiah O'Brien* was placed in mothballs in Suisun Bay, near San Francisco. Charged with dismantling the 300-ship fleet in 1962, Captain (later Admiral) Thomas J. Patterson was struck by the excellent appearance and overall condition of the *O'Brien* and decided to save her from destruction. Through his efforts and those of hundreds of volunteers, the *Jeremiah O'Brien* was refitted at the Bethlehem shipyard and returned to operating condition. Today she is berthed at the Maritime National Historic Park in San Francisco where she makes an annual cruise each Maritime Day.

The *John W. Brown* was launched at 12:12 P.M. on September 7, 1942, Labor Day, and was named for a prominent American labor leader. She departed two weeks later for the Persian Gulf with a cargo of tanks and ammunition bound for Russia. In June 1943, she was converted to a limited-capacity troopship and served in the Mediterranean transporting troops and cargo between North Africa and Sicily, the Italian mainland and France. The ship saw duty off the invasion beaches of Anzio, Salerno, and southern France.

After eight wartime voyages, the *Brown* continued carrying government cargoes to Europe, helping to rebuild the war-shattered continent. On December 13, 1946, the ship was given to the City of New York where she served until 1982 as a floating nautical high school, the only such ship of her kind in the United States. On March 1, 1985, the ship was listed on the National Register of Historic Places. She was towed to Baltimore in 1988 and dedicated as a Liberty Ship Memorial Museum in ceremonies held September 5, 1988.

The *John W. Brown* is available to the public, school groups, and organizations for tours, and the restoration of the *Brown* to operating condition allows her to make cruises on the Chesapeake Bay. The ship is maintained by Project Liberty Ship, a nonprofit volunteer organization.

Except for these two floating relics, the Liberty ships are gone, but the contributions made by the rapidly built vessels, the men and women who built them, and the men who sailed and defended them can never be forgotten or underestimated. Fifty years ago they made a vital and heroic "thin gray line" across the oceans, doing their part to crush worldwide aggression.

The "Ever Unlucky" Pandora

T HE NEWS OF MUTINY in the South Seas, aboard *H.M.S. Bounty*, shocked England and much of the rest of the civilized world. Lieutenant William Bligh and eighteen loyal officers and men of the *Bounty* had made an incredible open boat passage lasting forty-three days and covering 3,618 nautical miles to the island of Timor before their rescue; the survivors were welcomed home as heroes.

Bligh appeared before the Admiralty on March 16, 1790, to relate his tale. The Admiralty commended Lieutenant Bligh on his courage and resourcefulness and officially denounced the mutineers as "pirates." Because war with Spain seemed imminent, it was with some reluctance that the Admiralty assigned a warship to hunt down former Acting Lieutenant Fletcher Christian and the other mutineers in the far reaches of the South Pacific.

The ship chosen for the mission was *H.M.S. Pandora*, a three-masted, ship-rigged frigate armed with twenty-four guns and carrying a complement of one hundred-sixty officers and men. Given the massive buildup of a fleet for Lord Howe to lead against the Spanish, the manning and provisioning of the *Pandora* was not of primary

Lieutenant William Bligh captured the imagination of the civilized world with his story of treachery, mutiny and subsequent heroic fight for survival on the open seas.

concern, and it was some five months before a captain was even picked to lead the expedition.

Commanding officer of the *Pandora* was Captain Edward Edwards, a man as stern as his appearance suggested. At forty-nine he had served as post captain for nine years and had been employed in the Royal Navy for more then thirty years.

Captain Edwards's orders were explicit: to sail by way of Cape Horn directly to Matavai Bay, Tahiti, to search for the mutineers. If they were not on Tahiti, he was further instructed to expand his search throughout the Society and Friendly Islands. If he were to apprehend the "pirates," he was to "keep them as closely confined as may preclude all possibility of their escaping . . ." and "bring them to condign punishment."

Edwards was then to proceed to Endeavour Strait, between Australia and New Guinea, and return to England by way of the Cape of Good Hope. He would be partially successful in carrying out his orders, but not before losing his ship and a number of men.

Among the officers on board the *Pandora* were two lieutenants, Thomas Hayward and John Hallett, who had served as midshipmen aboard the *Bounty*. The ship's purser, Gregory Bentham, was also familiar with Tahiti, having sailed with Captain James Cook a few years before. To aid in the capture of the mutineers (and possibly to prevent any of *Pandora*'s crew from heeding the calls of the Tahitian sirens) a detachment of Marines joined the ship's company.

The ship sailed from Portsmouth on November 7, 1790. By the time she had cleared the English Channel, no fewer than thirty-five crewmen already had come down with a "malignant fever," in the words of ship's surgeon George Hamilton. The *Pandora* put in first at Tenerife and later at Rio to take on fresh provisions before rounding the Horn and entering the Pacific. The weather was fine, and the men's health began to improve.

Raising Tahiti on March 22, 1791, the *Pandora* received visitors on board as soon as she had dropped anchor in Matavai Bay the next day. Joseph Coleman, armorer for the *Bounty*, actually attempted to come on board even before the anchor was lowered, and *Bounty* midshipmen Peter Heywood and George Stewart boarded the *Pandora* and requested an audience with Captain Edwards.

They also asked to speak to their former shipmate, Lieutenant Hayward, who received them "coolly," as Heywood later wrote. Heywood and Stewart, along with several others, considered themselves innocent of any mutinous behavior, but Captain Edwards was to treat all of the surviving crewmen from the *Bounty* as criminals.

Edwards ordered Lieutenant Hayward not to discuss the case with his former messmates and had the two midshipmen immediately placed in irons. Four more former crewmen of the *Bounty* quickly gave themselves up and just as quickly found themselves clapped in irons. Lieutenants Hayward and Robert Corner were dispatched to locate the remaining eight crewmen who had been left on Tahiti. These unfortunate wretches eventually were apprehended without a struggle and brought on board the *Pandora*.

Two other mutineers, Charles Churchill and Matt Thompson, had quarreled earlier, resulting in Churchill's death at the hands of his crewmate. The Tahitians repaid Thompson for his villainy by pinning him to the ground with a branch and stoning him to death. As proof of his demise, some natives brought his severed head aboard the *Pandora* and presented it to Captain Edwards.

That accounted for sixteen of the "pirates" whom Edwards had been sent to find, but the ringleader, Fletcher Christian, and eight others were not to be found on Tahiti.

After setting Bligh and the loyal officers and men adrift, Mr. Christian and the others had returned to Tahiti for provisions and had tried in vain to establish a settlement on Toobouai. The natives there proved too hostile, and the *Bounty* returned once more to Tahiti. Sixteen of the men elected to stay there, while Christian, the rest of the mutineers, six Tahitian men, nineteen women, and a baby set sail for parts unknown.

Before he could begin his search for the remaining mutineers Edwards had to make provisions for his prisoners. Relating his actions to the Admiralty, Captain Edwards reported:

> I put the pirates into a round-house which I built on the after part of the quarter-deck, for their more effectual security in this airy and healthy situation, and to separate them from, and to prevent their having communication with, or to crowd and incommode, the ship's company.

James Morrison, boatswain's mate on the *Bounty* and now a prisoner aboard the *Pandora*, recalled it differently:

> The Carpenters were set to work to build a kind of Round-House . . . this place, which we stiled Pandora's Box, was only 11 feet in length and 18 feet wide . . . in which were two small Scuttles of 9 inches,

and one on the Top 18 or 20 inches square, secured with a bolt . . . the heat was so intense, that the Sweat . . . ran in Streams to the Scuppers, and soon produced Maggots. . . . This and two necessary Tubs which were kept in the Box, made it truly disagreeable. . . . This soon brought sickness among us. . . .

Likewise, Midshipman Heywood described the treatment of the prisoners in a letter to his mother: "There was a sort of prison built on the after-part of the quarter-deck, into which we were all put in close confinement with both legs and hands in irons, and were treated with great rigour." He added, "You may form some idea of the disagreeable situation I must have been in."

Sir John Barrow, who served as Second Secretary of the Admiralty for more than forty years, knew many of those involved and had access to voluminous official records. He wrote that Captain Edwards treated the prisoners "with rigour which could not be justified on any ground of necessity or prudence."

Nevertheless, the ship's surgeon, Dr. Hamilton, noted that Captain Edwards ordered that the inmates of Pandora's Box receive full rations instead of the two-thirds rations normally allotted to prisoners.

With fourteen of the alleged mutineers now secure under lock and key, Edwards began his search for the remainder of the mutinous crew, sailing from Tahiti on May 8, 1791, accompanied by a crew placed on board the schooner *Resolution* which had been built by former crewmen of the *Bounty*. Whereas Lieutenant Bligh had tarried six months in Tahiti, Captain Edwards had rounded up the mutineers, built a shipboard prison, provisioned his vessel, and sailed in six weeks.

Edwards had enjoyed considerable success up until the time he left Tahiti. Other than bouts of sickness among his crew, he had had relatively few problems. He had captured the majority of the alleged mutineers without losing a man, and he had furthered good relations with the native chieftains. But Captain Edwards's luck was about to change.

As *Pandora* and *Resolution* sailed from Tahiti, Matavai Bay was filled with canoes. Dr. Hamilton recalled that the natives mourned the departure of the Englishmen, baring their bodies, slashing their foreheads with shells, and smearing the blood on their shoulders and chests. Women held up tiny infants fathered by the prisoners and cried out in anguish.

Captain Edwards now began his fruitless search for Christian's party. The ships prowled through the Society Islands and then headed west to the Cook Islands. Some flotsam from the *Bounty* was discovered at Palmerston Island, and the search intensified. Not only was the *Bounty* not found (she had never, in fact, been there), but the *Pandora*'s jolly boat was lost with all hands.

Under the command of Midshipman John Sivall, the boat did not return to *Pandora* when recalled. Edwards searched for the small boat and her five-man crew for five days to no avail. With reluctance, the *Pandora* and *Resolution* sailed away.

The ships made for the Duke of York's Island, discovered "New Land" (the island of Nukunono), and then headed south to the Samoa group. In a heavy squall *Pandora* and *Resolution* were separated. The *Pandora* searched for the schooner for two days before giving up.

The *Resolution* crew had standing orders to rendezvous with the *Pandora* at Anamooka in the event they were separated, but when *Pandora* arrived at the island, there was no sign of the little schooner.

Further search for the *Resolution* turned up nothing, and on August 2, Captain Edwards decided to sail for England. His orders specified that he "examine and survey" Endeavour Strait, and the *Pandora* reached the Great Barrier Reef soon enough. Edwards began searching for a passage through the Strait.

On the morning of August 28, Lieutenant Corner was dispatched in the ship's yawl to investigate what looked to be a break in the reef. Corner signaled late that afternoon that he had discovered the passage. As the boat was hoisted on board, the *Pandora* struck the reef.

Afterward, Midshipman Heywood recounted: "The Pandora, ever unlucky, and as if devoted by heaven to destruction, was driven by a current upon the patch of a reef. . . ."

The wreck of the Pandora. *FROM A SKETCH BY MIDSHIPMAN PETER HEYWOOD, RN.*

Prisoner Morrison wrote that "while she was on the Reef she lost her rudder and received many severe & repeated strokes, in so much, that every one expected the Masts would go overboard."

It was a tense night for all on board, especially the manacled prisoners in the cramped Pandora's Box. Morrison and Heywood reported that some of the men managed in desperation to break free of their bonds, but Captain Edwards had them put in irons again. He also ordered the sentinels to shoot any man trying to escape.

Within ten minutes of striking the reef, the ship had taken four feet of water. By midnight, the ship was over the reef, but the damage was too great to be repaired.

The ship's four boats were lowered over the side and stocked with bread, water, and a few other meager provisions.

As the crew of the *Pandora* abandoned the sinking ship, the prisoners begged Captain Edwards for mercy. The ship's armorer and a corporal of the Marines were instructed to free the men but only had time to release two from their irons. A few others managed to break free before the ship heeled over. According to Midshipman Heywood:

> She now began to heel over to port so very much, that the master-at-arms, sliding overboard, and leaving the scuttle vacant, we all tried to get up, and I was the last out but three. . . . I succeeded in getting out, and was scarcely in the sea when I could see nothing above it but the cross-trees, and nothing around me but a scene of the greatest distress.

Midshipman Heywood was "stark-naked" as he struggled in the water. He grabbed a plank floating nearby and struck out for an island about three miles distant but soon found himself picked up by one of the ship's boats.

In all, thirty-four men drowned, four of them former members of the *Bounty*'s complement and two with manacles still on their hands. The ninety-nine survivors of the wreck, including ten prisoners, camped on a sandy key for three days, during which time Captain Edwards refused to allow the prisoners a tent or any clothes to cover themselves. The men, cooped up so long in the darkness of Pandora's Box, were susceptible to sunburn. The only way to protect themselves was to cover their bodies with sand, and they soon "appeared as if dipped in large tubs of boiling water," as Mr. Heywood wrote his sister.

On September 1, the four boats began a dangerous open-boat voyage for Timor—eerily following in the wake of the unfortunate Lieutenant Bligh.

For Lieutenant Hayward, this was the second such unlikely passage, and he must have wondered about the probabilities of finding himself in such similar circumstances on two successive voyages. While a hardship, the passage covered only 1,200 miles and lasted seventeen days, considerably less than Bligh's epic feat.

The party stayed at Timor for three weeks before sailing on a Dutch vessel to Samarang where they unexpectedly discovered the schooner *Resolution*, long given up as lost. The ship had made her way to Samarang where the crew of six Marines and a quartermaster, under the command of Midshipman Renouard and Master's Mate Oliver, had awaited the arrival of the *Pandora*. Only one man was lost, dying just a few days before the *Pandora*'s crew arrived.

At Batavia, the *Pandora*'s crew was divided among four Dutch ships for the passage home. At the Cape, Captain Edwards and the prisoners joined *H.M.S. Gorgon*, arriving in Spithead on June 19, 1792. For most of those who had sailed on the unlucky *Pandora*, their ordeal was over. For the alleged mutineers, it seemed, the arrival home was only the beginning.

The prisoners were duly court-martialed. Four of them were acquitted, the other six condemned to death. Of the six found guilty, however, the court recommended Midshipman Heywood and Boatswain's Mate James Morrison to His Majesty's Royal Mercy. William Muspratt was reprieved on a technicality, and three men were hanged on board *H.M.S. Brunswick*.

Heywood and Morrison were pardoned by king's warrant, just five days before their former crewmates were executed. Heywood returned to the service and eventually achieved the rank of captain. Morrison, too, returned to sea. He was killed fifteen years later when *H.M.S. Blenheim* went down in a gale off Madagascar.

As for Captain Edwards, he was court–martialed for the loss of the *Pandora*. While he had shown little regard for the lives of his prisoners, especially during the wreck, and poor judgment in provisioning the boats before the *Pandora* went down, the court was not concerned with these matters. Edwards was acquitted and continued his naval service, rising to the rank of rear admiral in 1799. He died in 1815 at the age of seventy-three.

Lieutenant
Izac's
Great
Escape

O N THE MORNING OF May 31, 1918, U.S. Navy Lieutenant Edouard V. M. Izac was sitting alone in his quarters aboard the convoy ship *President Lincoln*, eating his breakfast, when the first two torpedoes slammed into the ship.

The *U-90* had been trailing the convoy since the previous evening, ever since the escorting warships had departed. The little group of merchant ships had steamed from England on May 29, after offloading troops and materiel bound for the war. Sighting the German submarine, they had put on more speed and zigzagged throughout the night, hoping to elude the silent hunter.

As the *Lincoln*'s stern began to slip beneath the waves, her three sister ships sped off in the direction of New York. The former Hamburg-American Lines vessel was doomed, and the order was given to abandon ship. Lifeboats were lowered over the side, and men began striking out toward distant England.

The German sub prowled among the lifeboats, her officers and men on the lookout for the *Lincoln*'s skipper. When they reached his lifeboat, Lieutenant Izac (who, at the time spelled his name "Isaacs"), a junior officer who had commanded the guns on the ship's afterdeck, persuaded the Germans that he was the senior surviving officer. He calmly, and falsely, reported that the captain had gone "down with the ship," thus allowing the captain and other senior officers to avoid capture.

On board the *U-90*, Izac was greeted by its commander, Captain Remy, who granted him free run of the boat. He was treated with respect and courtesy by his enemies, and he took advantage of his limited freedom to learn everything that he could about the U-boat.

Lieutenant Izac experienced firsthand what it was like to undergo an attack by Allied warships when two U.S. destroyers detected the submarine and proceeded to depth-charge it. He listened closely to English-speaking officers, studied charts, and, during his five weeks of captivity aboard the *U-90*, gathered vital information on U-boat construction, cruising depth and maximum operational depth, German submarine patrol routes, length of patrols, rendezvous points, and return routes to the submarine pens at Wilhelmshaven.

Izac determined to escape, if possible, believing that his information would be vital to the war effort. The U-boats had proven their effectiveness throughout the war. Nearly a million tons of shipping had been destroyed by the underwater predators during the month preceding Lieutenant Izac's capture. Izac's familiarity with the subs' routines, strengths, and weaknesses could aid tremendously the anti-submarine effort being waged by the Allied navies.

The twenty-six-year-old officer got his opportunity to attempt escape on June 10 as the *U-90* cruised through a narrow bay between Sweden and Denmark, both neutral countries. With the shore within sight, Lieutenant Izac planned to jump overboard and swim to safety. The Germans discovered him topside, however, and forced him to return below.

Arriving at Wilhelmshaven, Izac was imprisoned aboard the German sub tender *Preussen* for several days before being transferred to a shoreside prison known as the Commandatur. He was held there two days and was then moved to a prison in Karlsruhe called the "Listening Hotel," because its windowless cells contained hidden microphones.

After spending a day in solitary confinement, Lieutenant Izac

Lieutenant Edouard V.M. Izac received the Medal of Honor for his daring escape from a German prisoner of war camp. PHOTO COURTESY U.S. NAVAL ACADEMY.

was subjected to hours of interrogation. He revealed nothing and was transferred to the Officer's Camp in the Zoological Gardens at Karlsruhe four days later.

Izac had been noted for both his "enviable reserve" and his "stubbornness" in his *Lucky Bag* biography in his final year at the U.S. Naval Academy in 1915. Now, three years later, he had displayed that same "remarkable ability to keep his mouth shut" during interrogation, and he would prove to be as stubborn as ever in his determination to escape from prison, despite overwhelming odds. As he said in a later interview, "I knew where the subs landed, and how they landed. I wanted to get back to Admiral [William S.] Sims in London," chief of U.S. naval forces in Europe.

The handsome young officer began making plans for an escape immediately. The prison camp housed one hundred-sixty Allied officers—British, Italian, French, and Serbian. One of the French aviators, Izac discovered, had a German fiancée who was willing to aid in an escape plan. Some of the officers had managed to bribe one of the guards into relaying messages between the woman and the aviator.

The date of the escape was set for July 4—Independence Day. Lieutenant Izac would go through the wire and make his way to the German woman's house before setting out for the Swiss frontier.

On July 3, however, the friendly guard was discovered by camp authorities, and the French aviator was questioned extensively. Patrols were doubled and the escape plan abandoned. A few nights later Izac was awakened, searched, and put aboard a train bound for yet another prison camp.

Two German soldiers, a sergeant and a corporal, guarded the naval officer on board a train filled with German soldiers. Escape looked impossible, but Izac had so far survived imprisonment with his streak of stubbornness intact.

The train was moving downhill and was beginning to pick up speed, but Lieutenant Izac understood from conversations around him that it was nearing its destination, a prisoner of war camp in Villingen. If he were going to make an attempt, now was the time.

One of his guards had fallen asleep, and when the other turned to speak to a third soldier, Izac dived out the open window. The train was rolling along between thirty and forty miles an hour. Izac landed hard, hitting his head and knees on the cross ties. His legs were cut so badly that he could not bend his knees, but he stumbled to his feet and began shuffling away as fast as he could. Behind him he heard the train grind to a halt.

German voices cried out, and then Izac heard the crack of rifle fire and the whine of bullets whipping past his head. He stopped and held up his hands in surrender, but when his captors reached him they beat him into unconsciousness with their rifles. The German corporal even broke the stock of his weapon, so savage were his blows.

The two guards jerked Izac to his feet and marched him double-time the remaining five miles to the prison camp, beating and kicking him all the way. Upon arrival at the prison he was warned by the camp commandant that if he attempted escape again, he would be shot. The guards tossed him into a bug-ridden cell where he lay for six days before being summoned to a court-marital.

Sentenced to two weeks in solitary confinement, Izac came out thirty pounds lighter and more determined than ever to escape and get his information to Allied authorities. Of the fifty attempted escapes from Villingen, however, only one had met with success. Nonetheless, Lieutenant Izac went to work on his plan.

He devised a plan to use a home-made ladder, climb on top of a work shed, jump to another roof, climb along the wire, and drop to freedom. The night of his planned escape, however, it rained. The next day, the camp guards began reinforcing the wire barricade.

Two more attempts were also foiled, and Izac suspected that the Russian officers in the prison camp were relaying his plans to their guards. Izac handpicked twelve American officers whom he trusted and told them of his latest plan. The men would split into four teams and would attempt to go over or cut through the fence simultaneously at four different locations.

The first team would use a stolen file to cut through the iron bars on the barracks window and use a piece of stolen wood as a bridge to pass from the barracks to the outer row of wire surrounding the camp. The second team would use its stolen wire cutters to breach the outer wire elsewhere. The third team would take advantage of the ensuing confusion to go out the main gate, while the fourth team would use a homemade ladder to go over the outer wire.

The bars in the window were cut on the afternoon of October 6, 1918, and, just after lights out at 10:30, one of the teams ripped down a set of electric wires, short-circuiting the entire prison camp. Izac slid the bridge, which had been blackened with shoe polish, out the window and onto the wire. As soon as it hit, a guard rushed to the area, but not before the three-man team had crossed to the outside.

Gunfire erupted as the men fled in different directions. No one was hit, and some of the men in the third team were able to rush out the main gate behind a group of forty German soldiers who began firing at Izac and his team members. One of the third team members who escaped was Lieutenant Harold Willis, an aviator from the famed Lafayette Escadrille. Willis met Izac at a predetermined rendezvous about two miles away, and they headed for the Swiss border.

The two men sprinkled pepper after them and waded along icy streams to confuse the dogs, covering about ten miles that first night. They traveled mostly at night, avoiding roads and bridges, living off raw vegetables stripped from farmers' fields. For six days and nights they avoided capture, walking about one hundred-twenty miles.

They reached the heavily patrolled Rhine River on the evening of October 12. After observing the border guards for about four hours, Izac and Willis crawled on their hands and knees down the bed of a mountain creek that flowed into the river.

Stripping off their clothes, the two stepped into the cold water and struck out for the opposite bank. The current swept Willis away, and Izac soon found that he didn't have the strength to fight the current. Just as he was about to give up, his feet touched sand. To his relief, Izac realized that he had reached Switzerland.

He found a farmhouse and sought shelter there. The next morning he was turned over to the Swiss authorities and was delighted to learn that Willis had also safely made it to freedom.

The two men were taken to Berne, interviewed by the American Commission for the Exchange of Prisoners of War, loaned money by the American Red Cross, and ordered to Paris. From there, Lieutenant Izac was ordered to London, where he briefed Admiral Sims on October 23. The British Admiralty questioned him for three days, and on November 2 he left England. The Armistice was signed nine days later.

For his outstanding services above and beyond the call of duty, Lt. Edouard Victor Michael Izac was awarded the Medal of Honor, the nation's highest military decoration. Assistant Secretary of the

Navy Franklin Delano Roosevelt presented the medal to Izac in a ceremony at the Washington Navy Yard.

Izac, promoted to lieutenant commander, retired from the Navy in 1921, due in part to wounds he had received while a prisoner of war. He went on to serve four terms in Congress as a representative from California. In later years he raised cattle and devoted his time to writing and travel.

Before he died in 1990 at the age of 98, Edouard Izac was the oldest living recipient of the Medal of Honor and the oldest living graduate of the Naval Academy.

The
Waving Girl
of
Savannah

IT HAS BEEN SAID many times that a sailor has a girl in every port, but there was once a girl who won the hearts of thousands of sailors for nearly fifty years. Most never knew her name, but she was famous the world over simply as "The Waving Girl."

Her name was Florence Martus, and by all accounts, she was a vivacious, pretty girl with fiery red hair. The daughter of a German immigrant, who had served in the U.S. Army at nearby Fort Pulaski for forty years before becoming the lighthouse keeper on Elba Island, Florence took a natural interest in the ships that sailed or steamed past her island outpost.

Upon the death of their father, Florence's brother, George Washington Martus, became keeper of the lights of the lower flats range below the mouth of the Savannah River. Florence took care of the lighthouse keeper's cottage, spending her time gardening and reading. As she worked among her flowers and vegetables, she would often wave to the passing vessels, inbound for Savannah or sailing for distant ports of call.

The slender young woman standing next to the trim white cottage, surrounded by flowering shrubs and bristling palmettos,

waving to strangers who might never see her again, made a romantic figure.

Sailors returning home to Savannah welcomed the girl's wave, knowing that they would soon be among family and friends. Those going to sea appreciated the wave as a last gesture of farewell until they could return safe and sound. Captains and pilots cheerfully returned Florence's greeting with a blast of their ship's horn.

It isn't known if she gave much thought to her simple, honest act

The bronze of Florence Martin by Felix DeWeldon greets every ship passing the Savannah waterfront. PHOTO COURTESY SAVANNAH AREA CONVENTION & VISITORS BUREAU.

of friendliness, but a letter from a man drove home the message that a wave from a stranger can have a powerful impact. A passenger on a steamer, long an expatriate, was the recipient of one of Florence's waves upon his return to America. For him, he wrote, the greeting had seemed a personal welcome, reserved for him after his long absence from home.

At that point, Florence determined to greet every ship that

passed Elba Island. And thus, in 1887, began the ritual that would make Florence Martus famous in distant ports as the Waving Girl.

She waved at every vessel on the river: fishing boats, tugs, coasters, and ocean–going carriers of every description. Rain or shine, she would wave a white handkerchief as the ship or boat floated past. Savannah's frequent summer showers did little to deter Florence. She would stand at the end of the house's piazza, sheltered from the rain, and wave.

The Waving Girl soon came to be expected by those who regularly plied the waters of the Savannah River, and her greeting always proved to be an unexpected pleasure to those who experienced it for the first time. Stacks of letters and packages from appreciative mariners arrived at the island for the Waving Girl, and Florence received gifts from all over the world, including many an exotic animal or bird picked up by admirers in the distant corners of the globe.

Sailors not only wrote to the Waving Girl expressing their gratitude: many wrote of missing her if their ship passed Elba Island at night. Accordingly, Florence began lighting a lamp every evening as the sun went down and would set it at the end of the piazza as darkness gathered. Whenever a ship would pass at night, Florence would swing the lantern in long arcs and hear the blast of the vessel's horn in return.

Florence devoted her life to waving to the passing ships. Not a vessel went past—no matter how small or large—that didn't receive a greeting from the Waving Girl, day or night. She became a fixture of the maritime world, as much as the Statue of Liberty in New York Harbor or, later, the Little Mermaid in Copenhagen. Yet, how much better—the Waving Girl was a real-live woman. For most she remained a mysterious figure, a slender woman in the distance, waving her white handkerchief to any and all who would look.

Not unsurprisingly, a number of legends grew up around the Waving Girl. A popular story told on board ships and in sailors' taverns around the world was that the Waving Girl once had a lover who had been lost at sea and that she waved at every passing ship in the hope her man would return. Another version suggested that the man in her life had simply sailed away, never to return. Still others insisted that the Waving Girl wasn't quite right, that she waved to ships due to some mental deficiency.

The truth is that the Waving Girl didn't have just one man in her life. She had thousands. She held every one of the officers and crewmen of the passing ships, as well as their passengers, dear to her heart. Over the years, numerous reporters trekked to Elba Island to interview the Waving Girl, and each came away charmed by her, sure of her sanity and enchanted by her devotion.

And though she never came into contact with most of those to whom she waved, the crew of one river vessel owed her more than just appreciation. At three o'clock one morning, Florence spotted a raging fire in the river, and she and her brother George immediately undertook a rescue operation.

Toiling back and forth between the island and the burning dredge in their little boat, Florence and George Martus saved the crew of the burning vessel, thirty men in all. Only one man died some time later, due to burns he had received.

The Waving Girl faithfully carried out her self-appointed duties for more than four decades. Her admirers never failed to sound their horns for her, even when violent squalls or heavy fog obscured her from their vision. They knew the Waving Girl was there, and it comforted them as they put to sea or neared the port.

The Waving Girl waved to her last ship in 1931 when George Martus retired as lighthouse keeper. Brother and sister left Elba Island and moved to Bona Bella, outside of Savannah.

She might have left her station at the lighthouse, but no one had forgotten the Waving Girl. When Florence Martus turned seventy, the city of Savannah threw an extravagant birthday party for their famous daughter. Some 3,000 people turned out for the party on Elba Island, with music provided by the U.S. Navy Band.

Miss Martus died in 1943, but her memory lives on. She is still on hand to greet all ships that sail past the Savannah waterfront. Walking past historic Factors Walk and winding one's way down to the cobblestone street that runs along the river, a visitor finds what Betsy Fancher described as "the most romantic figure on the waterfront," a handsome likeness of Miss Martus and her dog, cast in bronze, forever waving to the water traffic on the Savannah River. Chances are the Waving Girl would have liked it that way.

EDUCATED IN ENGLAND and the United States, Scott Rye is a Phi Beta Kappa, *cum laude* graduate of Rhodes College. His lifelong love of the sea led him to become a correspondent for an international daily shipping publication and editor of America's oldest port magazine, *Port of Mobile*.

Mr. Rye holds a commission in the U.S. Naval Reserve and is attached to a strike fighter squadron. He lives with his wife and daughter in Mobile, Alabama, where he works for the city's oldest advertising agency.